City *of* Readers

Portland Bookstores

1. Barnes and Noble Booksellers
2. St. Johns Booksellers
3. University of Portland Bookstore
4. Reflections Mirror-Image Bookstore ·
5. Talking Drum Bookstore
6. In Other Words
7. Bridge City Comics
8. Title Wave Used Bookstore
9. New Renaissance Bookstore
10. Twenty-Third Avenue Books
11. Audubon Society of Portland Nature Store
12. William Temple House Thrift Store
13. Daedalus Books
14. Trinity Episcopal Cathedral Bookstore
15. Great Northwest Bookstore
16. Oregon Health and Science University Bookstores
17. Annie Bloom's Books
18. Lewis & Clark Law School Bookstore
19. Lewis & Clark College Bookstore

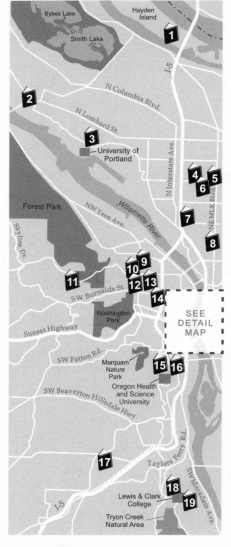

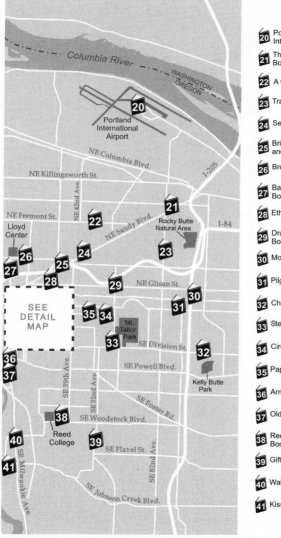

20 Powell's Books at Portland International Airport

21 The Grotto Christian Books and Gifts

22 A Children's Place

23 Trang's Books

24 Second Glance Books

25 Bridgetown Hobbies and Games

26 Broadway Books

27 Barnes and Noble Booksellers

28 Ethos

29 Dragon's Head Books and Gifts

30 Moyer's Bookstore

31 Pilgrim Discount

32 Christian Supply

33 Steiner Storehouse

34 Circuit Rider Books

35 Paper Moon Books

36 Armchair Bookstore

37 Old Friends Books

38 Reed College Bookstore

39 Gifts of the Spirit

40 Wallace Books

41 Kiss Books

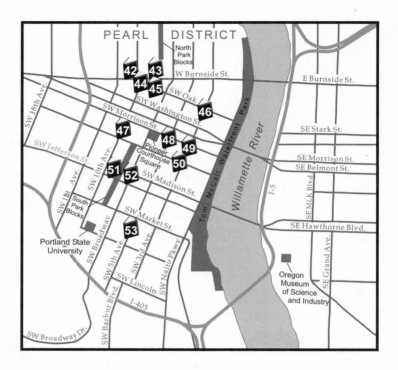

Downtown Bookstores

Powell's City of Books

Powell's Technical Books

Counter Media

Reading Frenzy

Cameron's Books and Magazines

Friends' Library Store

Borders Express

Borders

Looking Glass Bookstore

Portland Art Museum Store

Oregon Historical Society Museum Store

Portland State Bookstore

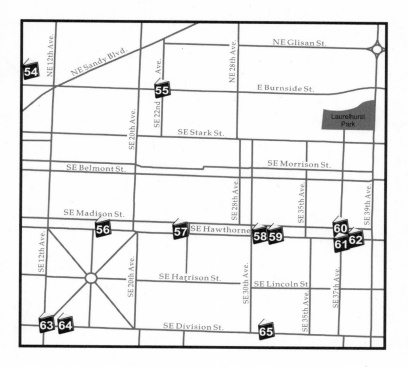

Inner Eastside Bookstores

54 Laughing Horse Books

55 Future Dreams Books

56 Agapé

57 Excalibur Books and Comics

58 Hawthorne Boulevard Books

59 Murder by the Book

60 The Needle

61 Powell's Books on Hawthorne

62 Powell's Books for Home and Garden

63 Alcoholics Anonymous

64 Longfellow's Bookstore

65 Serenity Shop

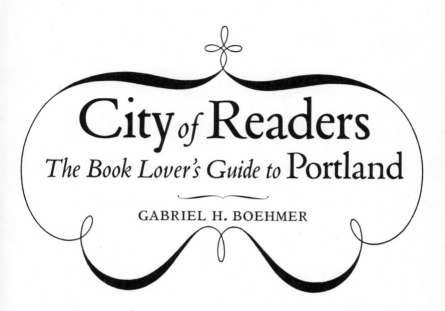

City of Readers
The Book Lover's Guide to Portland

GABRIEL H. BOEHMER

Tall
Grass
press

Tall Grass Press
P.O. Box 14036
Portland, OR 97293
www.tallgrasspress.com

"An Afternoon in the Stacks" is reprinted from *The Way It Is:
New and Selected Poems* with the permission of Graywolf Press,
Saint Paul, Minnesota.

Printed in the United States of America

Library of Congress Control Number: 2006932481
ISBN-13: 978-0-9785854-0-2
ISBN-10: 0-9785854-0-2

Every effort has been made to ensure the accuracy of the information
in this book. However, due to the ever-changing nature of business
operations, public transportation, and other specifics, it is recommended that you call ahead to verify an individual business's listing.
Neither the publisher nor the author can be held responsible for any
errors, omissions, or adverse consequences resulting from the use of
this book's content.

In memory of
George W. Boehmer (1891–1989)
&
G. R. "Bob" Boehmer (1913–1998)

An Afternoon in the Stacks

Closing the book, I find I have left my head
inside. It is dark in here, but the chapters open
their beautiful spaces and give a rustling sound,
words adjusting themselves to their meaning.
Long passages open at successive pages. An echo,
continues from the title onward, hums
behind me. From here the world looms,
a jungle redeemed by these linked sentences
carved out when an author traveled and a reader
kept the way open. When this book ends
I will pull it inside-out like a sock
and throw it back in the library. But the rumor
of it will haunt all that follows in my life.
A candleflame in Tibet leans when I move.

WILLIAM STAFFORD
from *The Way It Is: New and Selected Poems*

Contents

ACKNOWLEDGMENTS

THANKS TO THE MANY Portland readers, librarians, and book-sellers who generously shared their time, expertise, and passion for books with me. In particular, I am grateful for my agent, Bernadette Baker, who believed in me and this idea from the start, and for my publishers, Beth Caldwell Hoyt and Julie Steigerwaldt, who made it possible to do what I love. Special thanks to Carol Franks for her careful reading of the manuscript; to my wife, Jenny, whose name should probably appear on the cover as well; and to my son, Cameron, who kept asking me, "Are you having fun?"

INTRODUCTION

Portland's Love Affair with Books

IF YOU LOVE BOOKS—reading them, recommending them, borrowing them, collecting them, hearing their authors read them, discussing them, even mending them—Portland, Oregon, is your Mecca. Each day, thousands of readers make pilgrimages to the city's bookstores, libraries, campuses, and coffee shops to spend their leisure in the company of books and other readers.

Maybe Portland's abundance of rain is the culprit. As Swedish novelist Mikael Niemi says of his hometown, Pajala, the "extreme climate knocks the senses off kilter." Maybe Portland's wellspring of coffee is a conspirator. Maybe Portland's wealth of natural and man-made beauty attracts thoughtful people to visit and to live here. Whatever the reasons, there's no doubt about it: Portland has a torrid love affair with books.

In fact, Hennen's American Public Library Ratings places Multnomah County Library number two nationwide, among seventy-seven libraries in metropolitan areas with more than 500,000 residents.[1] Another study, "America's Most Literate Cities," which tallies total scores for cities with populations of 200,000 or more based on data from five categories—educational attainment, booksellers, newspaper circulation, library resources, and periodicals published— rates Portland number eleven, ahead of cities such as Philadelphia and New York.[2]

Portland is also host to the nation's best-attended author lecture series (Portland Arts and Lectures drew ten thousand in 2005), home of the country's largest independent bookstore (Powell's City of Books) plus a vibrant network of more than a hundred smaller shops, ranging from general stock to specialties such as mystery, feminism, graphic novels, radical politics, psychology, and spirituality.

City of Readers is the Portland book lover's Swiss Army Knife, including a selected directory of local bookstores and libraries, with commentaries on unique features and personalities—human, feline, and canine. In this book is a listing of the city's big literary events, such as the Wordstock festival and the Portland Arts and Lectures series, plus guides to more personal resources, such as reading groups,

1. Thomas J. Hennen Jr., *American Libraries*, Volume 36, Issue 9, October 2005, pages 42–48.

2. Dr. John W. Miller, President, Central Connecticut State University, "America's Most Literate Cities," www.ccsu.edu/amlc/.

lectures, courses, and volunteer opportunities. These pages are sprinkled with surprises, too. You'll find out where to splash alongside life-size versions of Beverly Cleary's Ramona Quimby, Henry Huggins, and Ribsy. *City of Readers* includes recommended reading lists: novels set in Portland, nonfiction about Portland, and a growing-by-the-day list of Portland authors.

For visitors to the City of Roses, new residents, or seasoned Portlanders who are unofficial travel guides, *City of Readers* is the shortest route to connecting readers with just the right reading opportunity. In a town where there's always a downpour of literary choices, *City of Readers* will lead you to the perfect cover.

PART ONE

Alone with Company:
Twenty-five Best Places to Read

PORTLAND TEEMS WITH SPOTS where you can be alone in the company of others: libraries, parks, cafés in restored turn-of-the-century buildings. The trick is finding the place that fits your reading personality. Do you like to be surrounded with lots of activity or little? Do you want the option of striking up a conversation, or do you want to be left alone? Are interior aesthetics important? Or is your top priority locally roasted, organic coffee?

The best place to read isn't always your own backyard. Especially if you live in Portland. Other than the rain and cold, there are other reasons that draw us to that strange relationship: being alone in the company of strangers. I don't know about you, but sometimes I would rather be anywhere besides alone at home. While I'm not necessarily looking for conversation, I'd like to have the opportunity for a chat, under certain circumstances—for instance, when I see someone reading John Kennedy Toole's *A Confederacy of Dunces*, Bernard Malamud's *A New Life*, or Clatskanie, Oregon, native Raymond Carver's *Will You Please Be Quiet, Please?* When you are an enthusiast of a book with a small following—and if you are a reader of literary fiction, any book you like probably fits that bill—sometimes you want to connect with another reader just to make sure you're sane. What has this to do with the best places to read in Portland? Only to say that if you prefer the solitude of your apartment, dorm, or house—or your backyard—that in fact is the best place to read. If you want to grab a book, and maybe a notebook and pen, and enjoy solitude in the company of others, there are many wonderful spots—indoors and outdoors—in the city. In most cases, the price is right: your ticket for admission is your own book. Nurse a coffee. Tip the person at the counter. The key to a pleasant outing is knowing your preferences: Do you want minimal or maximum exposure to others? Do you want noise or peace and quiet? Whatever your preferences, there's a spot just right for you. Without further ado, here are some of the best places, not in any sort of ranking:

MARK O. HATFIELD U.S. COURTHOUSE

Tuck a copy of Phillip Margolin's *The Associate* or Fred Leeson's *Rose City Justice* into your briefcase, ride up to the ninth floor of the building called "The Schick" (nicknamed for its convex roof that suggests the shape of a razor), and take a seat on the bench in the roof garden. (By the way, Portland's prolific Margolin—seven novels since he left his legal practice to write full-time in 1996—is a former criminal defense attorney who represented thirty homicide defendants, including several who faced the death penalty.) A stroll through the marble halls of the Hatfield Courthouse puts you in the perfect frame of mind to enjoy a legal thriller. Remember to bring photo ID.

1000 SW 3rd Ave. (between Southwest Salmon and Main streets). Hours: weekdays, 7 a.m. to 5 p.m.

PORTLAND STREETCAR

That's right, one of my favorite place to read *moves*. Your ideal travel companion is Kaie Wellman's *Eat Shop Portland*. Board at Portland State University's urban plaza (bordered by Southwest Mill and Montgomery streets between Fifth and Sixth avenues) for a forty-five-minute round trip through the Pearl District and back downtown. (If you're new to the city, it's a cheap alternative to a Grayline tour bus.) The comfortable seats and big windows replicate the experience of riding on a slow-moving train. There are also three big advantages to this moving easy chair: Central Library, Powell's and its Oak Street brethren (Reading Frenzy and Counter Media), and Twenty-Third Avenue Books. All are right on the streetcar line, which runs northbound on Southwest 10th Avenue and southbound on Southwest 11th Avenue between Southwest Montgomery and Northwest Northrup streets. Trains run about every fifteen minutes. Note to downtown cube dwellers: There's no better stress-breaker for a downtown worker–reader.

Especially on rainy days, it's a warm and cozy way to get out of the office.

TriMet Ticket Office at Pioneer Courthouse Square, 701 SW 6th Ave., 503-238-7433. Streetcar hours: Monday–Thursday, 5:30 a.m.– 11:30 p.m.; Friday, 5:30 a.m.–11:45 p.m.; Saturday, 7:15 a.m.–11:45 p.m.; and Sunday, 7:15 a.m.–10:30 p.m. Cost: $1.70, $1.35 for youth, and 85 cents for honored citizens; free between downtown and Northwest Irving Street.

TRIMET

The reason any TriMet bus or MAX (Metropolitan Area Express) Light Rail line makes a great place to read goes without saying: The characters you see and hear can rival the characters on the page. (If you're new to town, public transit is perfect vehicle for reading Chuck Palahniuk's *Fugitives and Refugees: A Walk in Portland, Oregon*.) Also on board: there's poetry that, if you pay attention, might just open a new world of reading to you. Carrie Hoops, former executive director of Literary Arts, brought to Portland the Poetry In Motion project that has enhanced the daily commutes of thousands of workers and travels of other passengers every day since 1997. Early mornings and late afternoons, TriMet buses are filled with commuter–readers, many of them students. Multnomah County Library books are frequent passengers, too. If you need to get out of the house, grab a book and catch the bus or train.

TriMet Ticket Office at Pioneer Courthouse Square, 701 SW 6th Ave., 503-238-7433.

PIONEER COURTHOUSE SQUARE

Noontime on a weekday is the perfect time to take your seat in the company of hundreds of others in downtown Portland's outdoor living room, weather permitting. It's an ideal place to take Portland's literary temperature by surveying what the crowd is reading. (By the way, J. Seward Johnson's bronze statue of a man holding an umbrella, *Allow Me*, is *not* the model for the *City of Readers* silhouette on the cover. That's a 1926 image of Congressman William D. Upshaw of Georgia, standing on a railing in front of the U.S. Capitol, from the vast collection of images in the Library of Congress Online Catalog at www.loc.gov.) If, like my wife, Jenny, you love to be at the center of the action, Pioneer Square is *the* place to read downtown—

PORTLAND'S LIVING ROOM—Grab a book and relax at Pioneer Courthouse Square. Mystery fans: See if you can find Sherlock Holmes among the names on the square's bricks.

visitors to the square total 7.7 million per year. Although Powell's Travel Store regrettably had to pull up stakes from its Pioneer Courthouse Square space, cutting off a handy selection of reasonably priced remainders, Powell's does hold a tented "Square Deal" sale each year. An ideal reading companion for your visit to Pioneer Courthouse Square is Bart King's *An Architectural Guidebook to Portland*.

701 SW 6th Ave. (between Southwest Morrison and Yamhill streets), 503-223-1613.

PORTLAND ART MUSEUM

Sometimes we prefer to read in the *quiet* company of others, and for this there's no better place than the Portland Art Museum. Plus, it's an inspiring place to read or write. The most economical way to add the museum to your regular reading routine is a tax-deductible $45 annual membership. Especially if you work or live downtown, the museum is a convenient destination for rainy weekday noontimes or cloudy weekend afternoons. Pick an out-of-the-way exhibit, pull out your book of poetry (I recommend Portlander Sandra Stone's *Cocktails with Brueghel at the Museum Cafe*), take a seat, and read away. My favorite hideaway at the museum, which doesn't require an admission fee, is the new Annie and James Crumpacker Family Library on the second floor of the Mark Building (formerly the Masonic Temple) in the wing closest to Main Street. Just check in at the reception desk inside the main entrance to the Mark Building.

1219 SW Park Ave. (Park is equivalent to 9th Avenue; entrance is closest to Southwest Jefferson Street), 503-226-2811. Hours: Tuesday, Wednesday, and Saturday, 10 a.m.–5 p.m.; Thursday and Friday, 10 a.m.–8 p.m.; Sunday, noon–5 p.m.

BASIL HALLWARD GALLERY

Here's a *free* alternative to the Portland Art Museum. Dash up to the third floor of Powell's City of Books and grab a seat on the Pearl Room's wooden benches, installed for viewing the Basil Hallward Gallery art exhibits. (The gallery is named for the portraitist in Oscar Wilde's novel *The Picture of Dorian Gray*.) This is the least-trafficked area of the store and a good bet for a quiet read, as long as there isn't an author event on tap. It's a roomy spot to explore an art book, such as Ginny Allen's *Oregon Painters: The First Hundred Years (1859–1959)*. And if you run into Michael Powell, he's a knowledgeable companion for a conversation about early Oregon painters, which he collects.

Inside Powell's City of Books, 1005 W Burnside St., 503-228-4651. Hours: daily, 9 a.m.–11 p.m.

FRESH POT

Portland is filled to the brim with independent coffee shops that are hospitable reading hangouts. The keys for me are finding cafés where the music doesn't overpower contemplation and the foot traffic is light. One of my haunts is Fresh Pot, inside

Powell's on Hawthorne (which, as a bonus, is the quirkiest store of Michael Powell's fleet, still small enough to be navigated thoroughly in thirty minutes). Fresh Pot offers several advantages: a counter facing Hawthorne Boulevard (perfect for a reader who wants to avoid eye contact and enjoy the colorful street scene); the aroma of freshly ground coffee in a small space; non-mall-clothed patrons; and the most positive-vibed owners around, Matthew "Vinnie" Vinci and David Columbo. Bonus: free WiFi, so when you find a book at Powell's, something a friend would die for, you can e-mail them. Bigger bonus: no cell phones. Biggest bonus: delicious, organic coffee in mismatched cups. Remember: cash only, and bring a dollar for a copy of *street roots*, the twice-monthly nonprofit newspaper that builds awareness about Portland's homeless issues, sold by a vendor outside Powell's.

3729 SE Hawthorne Blvd. (inside Powell's Books on Hawthorne), 503-232-8928. Hours: Monday–Thursday, 9 a.m.–10 p.m.; Friday–Saturday, 9 a.m.–11 p.m.; Sunday, 9 a.m.–9 p.m.

SEATTLE'S BEST

Location, location, location. MAX stops outside the floor-to-ceiling windows facing Yamhill. The hustle and bustle of the passengers makes you feel as if you're in a much larger city and provides a great backdrop for reading a gritty local book, such as Phil Stanford's *Portland Confidential: Sex, Crime, and Corruption in the Rose City*. Bonuses: contemporary art exhibitions, comfortable leather chairs.

708 SW 3rd Ave., 503-220-5911 (inside Border's at the Mohawk Building). Hours: Monday–Saturday, 9 a.m.–9 p.m.; Sunday, 10 a.m.–7 p.m.

BARNES AND NOBLE CAFE

I admit it: I go to the mall *sometimes*. Mostly for a walk down memory lane at Lloyd Center, one of my childhood hangouts. A quick trip around the ice rink mezzanine and a box of Joe Brown's caramel corn usually does the trick. However, if I need to kill some time while *other people to whom I'm related* are shopping, the café inside Barnes and Noble—with its signature mural of famous authors overhead—provides a safe harbor. But don't let me catch you reading anyone other than a local author.

1317 Lloyd Center (at Northeast Halsey Street and 12th Avenue), 503-249-0800. Hours: Monday–Saturday, 9 a.m.–10 p.m.; Sunday, 10 a.m.–7 p.m.

RIMSKY-KORSAKOFFEE HOUSE

Owned by Goody Cable, who also operates the literary-themed Sylvia Beach Hotel at Nye Beach in Newport, Oregon (a must-stay for booklovers, particularly the black-clad Edgar Alan Poe room, complete with guillotine suspended from the ceiling—more details available at www.sylviabeachhotel.com). Rimksy-Korsakoffee House serves coffee and dessert in the evening along with live classical music. Cash or check. For a flavorful slice of

Portland cultural history while you're there, nibble on a copy of the *The Rimsky Chronicles and Operating Manual: An Anthology* by Gillian Nance.

707 SE 12th Ave. (at Southeast Alder Street), 503-232-2640. Hours: Friday–Saturday, 7 p.m.–1 a.m.; Sunday–Thursday, 7 p.m.–midnight.

VILLAGE COFFEE

At the eastern border of Multnomah Village, this small shop sits just down the street from popular Annie Bloom's Books. There's organic coffee, friendly hosts who don't wear matching green aprons, free WiFi, and only four tables and a row of theater seats with a view of colorful Multnomah Boulevard. For $1.80, you get a seat and big cup of Joe. Refills 50 cents. Cash only. While you're here, dig into *Portland's Bounty: A Guide to Eating Locally and Seasonally in the Greater Portland and Vancouver Areas* by Jenny E. Holmes or *VegOut Vegetarian Guide to Seattle and Portland* by George Stevenson.

7781 SW Capitol Highway, 503-244-3954. Hours: Monday–Friday, 6:30 a.m.–8 p.m.; Saturday–Sunday, 7 a.m.–8 p.m.

CHAPMAN SQUARE PARK AND LOWNSDALE SQUARE PARK

It's the Central Park reading experience in downtown Portland. Wooden benches line the X-shaped walkways of the Plaza Blocks, attracting enough relaxed observers to balance the frenetic traffic. Break out your newspaper or paperback at lunch. You'll be in the company of attorneys scurrying between courthouses, roped lines of day-care kids, and aggressive pigeons. If you can find it at a used bookshop, pick up *Portland's Public Art: A Guide and History* by Norma Catherine Gleason and Chet Orloff, a slender volume that features delightful hand-drawn maps.

Southwest 4th Avenue between Salmon and Madison streets. More information and photos of both parks at www.portlandonline.com/parks/finder and from Portland Parks and Recreation, 1120 SW 5th Ave., Suite 1302, 503-823-7529.

SOUTH PARK BLOCKS AND NORTH PARK BLOCKS

In the heart of the cultural district on the southwest side, and bordering the Pearl and Historic Waterfront districts on their shorter northwest extension, the paths of the Park Blocks are bordered with excellent reading benches. A natural umbrella of European beech, American elm, Northern red oak, and London planetree provides year-round cover for readers. (*Trees of Greater Portland* by Phyllis C. Reynolds and Elizabeth F. Dimon includes the South Park Blocks as one of its "Nine Tree Tours" in the appendix.) Pick a spot south of the Portland Art Museum for maximum tranquillity. Enjoy watching the Portland State University crowd pass back and forth. Close your eyes, and you're transported back to your undergraduate days. Proximity to Portland Streetcar, MAX Light Rail, Oregon Historical Society, and Multnomah County Central Library.

South Park Blocks: Southwest Park Avenue between Market and Salmon streets. North Park Blocks: Northwest Park Avenue between Ankeny and Glisan streets. More information and photos of both Park Blocks at www.portlandonline.com/parks/finder and from Portland Parks and Recreation, 1120 SW 5th Ave., Suite 1302, 503-823-7529.

CENTRAL LIBRARY

The maps room on the third floor is your ticket to reading serenity—that, and a copy of *Art and Architecture in the Central Library*, an elegant booklet published by the Library Association of Portland in 1980. To redouble your enjoyment of this grand building, check out *Central Library: Portland's Crown Jewel* by Richard E. Ritz. Really, there are not many patrons reading maps all at once, so the maps room is one of the quietest spots in the library. Plus you can eat treats from Voodoo Doughnut (22 SW 3rd Ave.) for the rest of the day because you walked up three flights of stairs. (There's elevator access, too.) Also on the third floor, the benches in the Collins Gallery near the top of the stairs are a good spot. And for the most aesthetically pleasing experience, visit the John Wilson Room, a special collection that requires you to fill out a short registration and present photo identification.

801 SW 10th Ave. (between Yamhill and Taylor streets), 503-988-5123. Hours: Monday, 10 a.m.–6 p.m.; Tuesday–Wednesday, 10 a.m.–8 p.m.;

Thursday–Saturday, 10 a.m.–6 p.m.;
Sunday, noon–5 p.m.

DAILY CAFÉ AT REJUVENATION

The wall-sized map of early 1890s Portland neighborhoods sets the mood for reading about the city's history, so bring along Eugene Snyder's *Portland Names and Neighborhoods: Their Historic Origins* or William J. Hawkins III's *Classic Houses of Portland, Oregon: 1850–1950*. The café's stenciled tile floor might inspire your own remodeling idea. If lightning strikes, head to adjacent Rejuvenation, a locally owned period lighting and restoration hardware store. There you'll find a wheelbarrow full of titles about home projects, landscaping, and architecture.

1100 SE Grand Ave. (at Taylor Street), 503-234-8189.
Hours: Monday–Friday, 7 a.m.–4 p.m.; Saturday, 9 a.m.–4 p.m.;
Sunday, 11 a.m.–4 p.m.

STUMPTOWN COFFEE ROASTERS

The best of Portland in a nutshell—or in this case, a bean: locally roasted, organic coffee served in renovated spaces. Could it get any better? Yep. This locally owned business also serves free WiFi at each location. Of the three coffeehouses, downtown is my favorite reading spot: the big open space swallows the din of its devoted French press crowd. Third and Ash sells a big selection of magazines, too. The books to bring here are clear: Eugene Snyder's *Early Portland: Stump-Town Triumphant, Rival Townsites on the Willamette, 1831–1854*; and Robert Dietsche's *Jumptown: The Golden Years of Portland Jazz, 1942–1957*.

128 SW 3rd Ave. (at Ash Street), 503-295-6144,
Monday–Saturday, 7 a.m.–9 p.m.; Sunday, 7 a.m.–8 p.m.;
3356 SE Belmont St., 503-232-8889, Monday–Friday, 6 a.m.–9 p.m.;
Saturday–Sunday, 7 a.m.–9 p.m.; and 4525 SE Division St.,
503-230-7702, Monday–Friday, 6 a.m.–7 p.m.;
Saturday–Sunday, 7 a.m.–7 p.m.

KEN'S ARTISAN BAKERY

The aroma is haunting. You'll find yourself thinking about it hours after you've left. For the best of all possible worlds, browse through Portland's most aesthetically appealing bookstore, Daedalus, next door, where the aroma infuses the aisles. Small space, active crowd. It's best for readers who like the full sensory experience. The subject of Ursula K. Le Guin's *Blue Moon over Thurman Street* is within walking distance.

338 NW 21st Ave. (at Flanders Street), 503-248-2202. Hours:
Monday, 7 a.m.–6 p.m.; Tuesday–Friday, 7 a.m.–7 p.m.; Saturday,
7 a.m.–5 p.m.; Sunday, 8 a.m.–5 p.m.

TRUE BREW ESPRESSO

Every neighborhood should be so lucky to have a locally owned place like True Brew Espresso. It's also the perfect example of why you should take your brain off autopilot and venture somewhere new. Here's a pearl in the city's southeast Brooklyn neighborhood, inside Old Friends Books, where you can browse among the ten thousand volumes on the floor, enjoy a cup of locally roasted, organic coffee from Coffee Bean International, and read in a comfortable chair while you listen to classical music. Family friendly, Old Friends was made for reading a local resource book like *Out and About Portland with Kids: The Ultimate Family Guide for Fun and Learning* by Nelle Nix.

3370 SE Milwaukie Ave. (just south of Powell Boulevard), 503-231-9992. Hours: daily, 10 a.m.–6 p.m.

REED COLLEGE

Walking on this Southeast Portland campus puts you in an Ivy League state of mind, so bring a classic and, weather permitting, read on the bench shaped like a couple holding hands, just west of the Educational Technology Center. Weather forbidding, sit inside the Lilliputian Paradox Lost Café. Inside the Reed College Library is a tall and narrow reading room on the Main Level next to the South Stacks. If you haven't already, must-reads while you're here include John Reed's *Ten Days That Shook the World* and Louise Bryant's *Six Red Months in Russia*. (*Six Red Months* is available from the Oregon Cultural Heritage Commission in conjunction with Powell's Press.)

3203 SE Woodstock Blvd., 503-771-1112.

CAMPUS ESCAPE—Reading needn't be a solitary pursuit. Bring a friend and your books to this Reed College bench, near the Educational Technology Center.

CARNEGIE LIBRARIES

Sometimes a great place to read is created by a sense of history or its sheer beauty. Both are the case at any of the four Carnegie libraries in Portland: St. Johns Library, North Portland Library, Belmont Library, and Albina Library (now Title Wave Used Bookstore, operated by Multnomah County Library). These four branches are the legacy of philanthropist Andrew Carnegie, who donated $40 million to build 1,679 public libraries across the United States between 1883 and 1929. If you're looking for a great place to read yet haven't a book or periodical to bring along, the Portland Carnegies are your ticket. For wonderful reading at any library, try the second volume of Beverly Cleary's memoir, *My Own Two Feet*, which includes recollections of her years as a librarian.

St. Johns (7510 N. Charleston Ave., 503-988-5397), North Portland (512 N. Killingsworth St., 503-988-5394), Belmont (1038 SE 39th Ave., 503-988-5382), and Title Wave Used Bookstore (216 NE Knott St., 503-988-5021). Hours for all of the library branches: Monday, 10 a.m.–6 p.m.; Tuesday–Wednesday, noon–8 p.m.; Thursday–Saturday, 10 a.m.–6 p.m.; Sunday, noon–5 p.m. Title Wave Used Bookstore hours: Monday–Saturday, 10 a.m.–4 p.m.

BEVERLY CLEARY CHILDREN'S LIBRARY

If you want to inspire young readers, one of the best places for them to enjoy reading is the Beverly Cleary Children's Library at Central Library, where they can sit under the branches of the fourteen-foot-tall tree sculpture, whose bark combines images from Oregon's natural history with subjects found in the Dewey Decimal System. The bark also features toys, animals, musical instruments, letters, and storybook characters. While your young reader is paging through the leaves, dip into Portlander Ursula K. Le Guin's illustrated *Catwings* and *Catwings Return*.

---

801 SW 10th Ave. (between Yamhill and Taylor streets), 503-988-5123. Hours: Monday, 10 a.m.–6 p.m.; Tuesday–Wednesday, 10 a.m.–8 p.m.; Thursday–Saturday, 10 a.m.–6 p.m.; Sunday, noon–5 p.m.

HOLLYWOOD LIBRARY

If your young readers are Beverly Cleary fans, take them to read in the library at the heart of the neighborhood where Henry Huggins and Ramona books are set: Hollywood Library, just north of Sandy Boulevard. Kids can read in the children's section, within view of the wall-size map of Beverly Cleary's neighborhood, complete with landmarks such as Ramona Quimby's house at Northeast 28th and Klickitat, Ellen Tibbit's house at Northeast 33rd and Tillamook, and Laurelwood (Laurelhurst, really) Park at East Burnside and Northeast 33rd. Must read for grown-up Pest fans: Cleary's two-volume biography, *Girl from Yamhill* and *My Own Two Feet*.

4040 NE Tillamook St., 503-988-5391. Hours: Monday–Tuesday, 10 a.m.–8 p.m.; Wednesday–Saturday, 10 a.m.–6 p.m.; Sunday, noon–5 p.m.

THE GROTTO

For the spiritually minded and for those who enjoy reading outdoors, The Grotto (also known as the National Sanctuary of Our Sorrowful Mother) features an outdoor chapel with a majestic stone cliff backdrop. You can sit and read on parklike benches or pay for an elevator lift to the upper grounds where you can read in the quiet gardens. Perfect fit: *Two Voices: A Father and Son Discuss Family and Faith* by Portlander Brian Doyle and his father, Jim Doyle.

8840 NE Skidmore St. (at Northeast Sandy Boulevard and 85th Avenue), 503-254-7371. Hours: daily, opens at 9 a.m.; November (after Thanksgiving)–January, closes at 4 p.m.; February–May (up to

TRUNKFUL—As many books as a young reader's arms will carry are available at the Beverly Cleary Children's Library. The fourteen-foot bronze tree captivates book lovers of all ages.

the Saturday before Mother's Day), closes at 5:30 p.m.; May (beginning on Mother's Day)—September, closes at 7:30 p.m.; September (after Labor Day)—November (up to Thanksgiving), closes at 5:30 p.m.

SHAKESPEARE GARDEN

Washington Park in Portland's West Hills offers many idyllic places to read, none finer than the stone bench in the Shakespeare Garden in the southeast corner of the International Rose Test Garden. Dedicated in 1945, the Shakespeare Garden was originally designed to include only herbs, trees, and flowers mentioned in Shakespeare's plays. Today, the garden also includes roses named after his characters. For a list of plants mentioned in Shakespeare's plays, in addition to a compendium of his rose quotes, visit www.rosegardenstore.org. Plan a trip to the John Wilson Room at Central Library to see its large collection of rose materials, including *Roses at Portland, Oregon, and How to Grow Them: Papers and an Address* by F. V. Holman and W. S. Sibson. (The collection of rose materials is beautifully interpreted by local artist Deborah DeWitt Marchant in her pastel "Discoveries," available as a greeting card at the Friends' Library Store, located just inside the Central Library entrance.)

400 SW Kingston Ave., 503-823-3636.

PENINSULA PARK

Portland's most-beautiful rose garden is in North Portland, and it's a great place to read. Sit around the fountain and drink in the garden's beauty: 8,900 plantings on a two-acre site. Breathtaking when in bloom and free, free, free. At Central Library, ask to see *A Guide to Portland's Historic Parks and Gardens*, produced by the Junior League of Portland, Oregon, and the Oregon Preservation Resource Center.

700 N Portland Blvd., just west of Interstate 5.

Note to readers: If you'd like to share a great place to read not listed here, please visit the *City of Readers* Web site, www.cityofreaders.com, and post a note in the "Best Places" forum. You might even find your recommendation in the next edition of this book.

PART TWO

Read Locally: Authors and Books

A FUNNY THING HAPPENED on the way to the *City of Readers*. I thought it would be fun—I believe that was the exact word: *fun*—to include a checklist of Portland authors and their books, roughly from the dawn of time until now, companioned with similar lists of novels set in Portland and nonfiction books about Portland. After all, what better way for readers to get acquainted with the City of Roses than through the eyes of its authors and their books?

So I started asking readers, librarians, and booksellers the question "Who's your favorite Portland author?" And what happened can only be described as overwhelming. I thought I could fairly accurately predict the results. Portlanders over forty would probably answer, not necessarily in this order: Ursula K. Le Guin (*A Wizard of Earthsea*), William Stafford (*Traveling through the Dark*), Katherine Dunn (*Geek Love*), and Phillip Margolin (*Gone, But Not Forgotten*). Those under forty would answer: Chuck Palahniuk, Chuck Palahniuk, and Chuck Palahniuk (*Fight Club*). I might stumble upon an occasional Chuck Palahniuk, Chuck Palahniuk, and Charles D'Ambrosio (*The Point: And Other Stories*). And if I asked a twenty-something or something-teen, the end of the Chuck string might include Zoe Trope (*Please Don't Kill the Freshman*).

What a naïve, contemporary-fiction-centered reader I turned out to be! The maelstrom of suggestions began with a librarian—cleverly disguised as a reference librarian, yet who in fact was really a children's librarian—who answered my question with her own: "Are you going to include children's authors?" The benevolent authority of Susan Smallreed's voice warned I dare not answer: "You mean, there are children's authors from Portland other than Beverly Cleary?" This librarian's top-of-mind list beyond our beloved creator of *Ramona the Pest* was dizzying: Nancy Coffelt, David Gifaldi, Pamela Smith Hill, Eric Kimmel, Sara Ryan, Graham Salisbury, David Michael Slater. This Northwest Branch librarian then zipped into an online vault of local children's authors and rattled off even more Portlanders and Oregonians who are young readers' writers and illustrators.

The next blow to my worldview came from the proprietors of Excalibur Books and Comics, who led me to reading my first graphic novel, *Blankets*, by Midwest expatriate and Portlander

Craig Thompson, the heartthrob of graphic novel readers nation-wide. Proprietors Peter Fagnant and his daughter Debbie Fagnant also described Portland as a hotbed for comics writers (Brian Michael Bendis, *Ultimate Spider-Man*; Kurt Busiek, *Conan*; and Greg Rucka, *Gotham Central*), not to mention publishers (Oni Press and Top Shelf Productions in the city; Dark Horse Comics in nearby Milwaukie).

Meanwhile, a national epicenter of self-published zines is located on the Acorn Block, kitty-corner from Powell's City of Books, at the nonprofit Independent Publishing Resource Center, where readers can tap into *five thousand independently published* publications that are housed and catalogued at the IPRC library (see pages 66 and 152).

So, dear reader, although it would be impossible to list all Portland authors in these modest pages, I *can* offer you this: a selected list of titles by Portland authors in a few broad categories as well as several online resources that will keep you knee-deep in titles by Portland and Oregon authors until the end of time. Some of the titles are out of print. *Rats—that might mean an afternoon browsing the used-book stores.*

However, when looking for information about Portland authors and their books, you'll find the best sources of information, not to mention the most interesting and, likely, the most entertaining, to be other readers, your nearest librarian, or an independent bookseller. You might start the conversation like this: "Can you recommend a good book by a Portland author?" Come equipped with a tape recorder if you want to keep up with the answers.

Note: *City of Readers* follows the lead of the Oregon Library Association in selecting writers for the latter's *Oregon Authors* bibli-ography, available at www.olaweb.org/or-authors. To be considered for the following Portland lists, the author must have been living or working in Portland during the time the book was written, and the title must be catalogued on a major bibliographic database, such as Multnomah County Library, the Oregon State Library, or the Library of Congress. Categories of writing that are typically excluded include individual poems, textbooks, technical works, periodical articles, research papers, and esoteric materials.

To suggest your personal favorites, please visit the *City of Readers* Web site, www.cityofreaders.com.

► Novels and Mysteries Set in Portland

RANDY ALCORN. *Dominion* (1996). Best-selling Christian mystery novel and sequel to Alcorn's *Deadline* (1994), *Dominion* is the story of Clarence Abernathy, an Oregon columnist, who is dragged into the world of inner-city gangs and racial conflict. Alcorn, who lives in Gresham, Oregon, is founder and director of Eternal Perspectives Ministries. He has authored twenty books, including six novels.

KATHERINE DUNN. *Geek Love* (1989). This daring novel was nominated for the National Book Award. It's the first thing you should read when you arrive in the City of Roses—if you love it, you'll fit right in. Dunn, a onetime *Willamette Week* columnist who was the Story Lady for independent radio station KBOO, hatched the idea for her story about the Benewskis, a carnival family that breeds its own freaks, in the Rose Garden at Portland's Washington Park. See the special binding of *Geek Love*, illustrated and bound by Marc Blocker, at Central Library's John Wilson Room.

JAMES FOGLE. *Drugstore Cowboy* (1990). The story of four addicts who steal narcotics from Pacific Northwest pharmacies. The National Society of Film Critics voted the movie, directed by Portlander Gus Van Sant, best film of 1989.

ERNEST HAYCOX. *Long Storm* (1946). A Civil War–era novel about Portland as a booming frontier town with five thousand people and fifty-five saloons. Haycox was a native Portlander who attended Lincoln High School and graduated from the University of Oregon. Haycox wrote twenty-four novels and nearly three hundred short stories and kept regular hours at a downtown Portland office. Must read: "Tall Tales, True Tales: Ernest Haycox and Researching the Old West" by Ernest Haycox, Jr., in the fall 2003 issue of *Oregon Historical Quarterly*.

APRIL HENRY. *Buried Diamonds* (2003); *Circles of Confusion* (1999); and *Square in the Face* (2000). These mysteries are all part of Henry's series that feature Claire Montrose, a mousey Portland motor vehicles department worker turned sleuth. *Circles of Confusion* earned Agatha Award and Anthony Award nominations for best first novel.

KATY KING. *City of Suspects* (2003). From her office in downtown Portland's Galleria Building, private eye Jane Lanier tracks down the murderer of Federico DeOrca, an alleged mobster. This is the first novel by King, a Portlander who attended Madeline Elementary School and St. Mary's Academy and earned an English degree at the University of Oregon.

JEWEL LANSING. *Deadly Games in City Hall: A Murder Mystery* (1997). Lansing, who has served as auditor for the City of

Portland and Multnomah County, brings an insider's view to a political whodunit set in Portland.

URSULA K. LE GUIN. *The Lathe of Heaven* (1971). Meet George Orr, a man who can dream things into being, and experience a Portland where the greenhouse effect has pushed the annual rainfall total to 114 inches. This is Le Guin's seventh novel, and her only novel to date set in Portland.

PHILLIP MARGOLIN. *After Dark* (1995); *The Associate* (2002); *Gone, But Not Forgotten* (1993); *The Last Innocent Man* (1981); *Lost Lake* (2005); *Sleeping Beauty* (2004); *Ties That Bind* (2003); and *The Undertaker's Widow* (1998). Thorny (as in sharp) legal thrillers set in the City of Roses. All of the former Oregon criminal defense lawyer's novels have been *New York Times* bestsellers. To get hooked, start with *Gone, But Not Forgotten*.

► Nonfiction about Portland

CARL ABBOTT. *Greater Portland: Urban Life and Landscape in the Pacific Northwest* (2001). Abbott, a Portland State University professor of Urban Studies, examines the question of how Portland has achieved its reputation as one of the most progressive and livable cities in the United States.

BRIAN BOOTH, editor. *Wildmen, Wobblies and Whistle Punks: Stewart Holbrook's Lowbrow Northwest* (1992). A collection of twenty-six historic, colorful Northwest stories—tales of loggers and profiles of lowbrow characters—by Holbrook, the high school dropout who became one of the country's most popular historians and a satirical painter. Booth's introduction is a must-read for anyone interested in Northwest history.

JOHN FITCHEN. *Birding Portland and Multnomah County* (2004). Includes descriptions of ten primary and twenty-five associated birding sites.

LAURA O. FOSTER. *Portland Hill Walks: Twenty Explorations in Parks and Neighborhoods* (2005). The author, a longtime Portlander, maps out several expeditions through each section of the city. Routes include Linnton to Forest Park, Lair Hill to Oregon Health and Science University, Leach Botanical Garden to Mount Scott, and Willamette Cove to the St. Johns Bridge.

NORMA CATHERINE GLEASON AND CHET ORLOFF. *Portland's Public Art: A Guide and History* (1983). This charming, slender guide to the history and locations of the city's public art is begging to be updated.

CHRISTOPHER A. GOSSETT. *Portland's Historic Sidewalk Signatures: A Collection of 276 Rubbings of Builders Names and Construction Dates Stamped into Portland's Sidewalks from 1900 to 1930* (1983). This small volume is the perfect companion for urban walks—and an inventive way to introduce young Portlanders to the city's history. Grab butcher paper and crayons and take to the streets.

WILLIAM J. HAWKINS III AND WILLIAM F. WILLINGHAM. *Classic Houses of Portland, Oregon: 1850–1950* (1999). Hawkins, an architect, and Willingham, a historian, describe and illustrate more than three hundred of Portland's outstanding houses, including twenty-three distinct architectural styles.

MICHAEL HOUCK AND M. J. CODY. *Wild in the City: A Guide to Portland's Natural Areas* (2000). More than eighty-five maps and guides to natural sites in local watersheds as well as essays by Northwest writers, including Robin Cody and Kim Stafford.

MARCY COTTRELL HOULE. *One City's Wilderness: Portland's Forest Park* (second edition, 1996). A history and guide to the city's five-thousand-acre urban forest, with directions for twenty hikes of varying lengths, difficulty, and scenery.

ROBERT D. JOHNSTON. *The Radical Middle Class: Populist Democracy and the Question of Capitalism in Progressive Era Portland, Oregon* (2003). Winner of the President's Book Award from the Social Science History Association.

BART KING. *An Architectural Guidebook to Portland* (2001). An entertaining, informative read that's not too big to tote on a walk. Photos and short descriptions of the city's most prominent and some of its most unusual buildings.

JEWEL LANSING. *Portland: People, Politics, and Power, 1851–2001* (2003). Written by a former City of Portland and Multnomah County auditor, this is the definitive book about the city's political, social, and cultural history.

URSULA K. LE GUIN. *Blue Moon over Thurman Street* (1993). With black-and-white photographs by Roger Dorband, Le Guin reflects on the Northwest Portland street where she has walked for several decades.

E. KIMBARK MacCOLL. *The Growth of a City: Power and Politics in Portland, Oregon, 1915–1950* (1979); *Merchants, Money and Power:*

The Portland Establishment, 1843–1913 (1988); and *The Shaping of a City: Business and Politics in Portland, Oregon, 1885–1915* (1976). Three invaluable references that belong on the bookshelf of every serious student of Portland history, commerce, and politics.

RICHARD MARLITT. *Nineteenth Street* (revised edition, 1978). A photographic collection of houses on the Northwest Portland street that was once the city's most elegant avenue, from Burnside to Marshall.

GILLIAN NANCE. *The Rimsky Chronicles and Operating Manual: An Anthology* (1998). A collection of stories about the Rimsky-Korsakoffee House in Southeast Portland.

CHUCK PALAHNIUK. *Fugitives and Refugees: A Walk in Portland, Oregon* (2003). Essays by the author of *Fight Club* about off-the-beaten-path Portland, including a self-cleaning house, haunted spots around town, odd museums, and the downtown tunnel system. Includes a handy list of landmarks for photo-ops.

PAUL PINTARICH. *History by the Glass: Portland's Past and Present Saloons, Bars, and Taverns* (1996). Pintarich, a longtime reporter and book-review editor for *The Oregonian*, profiles the city's older taverns and saloons, such as The Alibi, Kelly's Olympian, Pal's Shanty, and the White Eagle.

PHYLLIS C. REYNOLDS AND ELIZABETH F. DIMON. *Trees of Greater Portland* (1993). A pictorial tour of 132 local trees, selected for their size, beauty, rarity, or history. Nine tree tours around town include the South Park Blocks, Reed College, and Sauvie Island.

RICHARD E. RITZ. *Central Library: Portland's Crown Jewel* (2000). An illustrated history that traces the library's founding through its 1997 renovation.

EUGENE E. SNYDER. *Portland Names and Neighborhoods: Their Historic Origins* (1979). An essential reference to resolve historical disputes among Portland know-it-alls. Learn how to pronounce "Glisan" like a native of this city.

PHIL STANFORD. *Portland Confidential: Sex, Crime, and Corruption in the Rose City* (2004). Stanford, a veteran contributor to the *Portland Tribune* and *The Oregonian*, uncorks the city's great vice scandal of the 1950s.

SHARON WOOD WORTMAN. *The Portland Bridge Book* (second edition, 2001). An illustrated book that contains fascinating facts about seventeen spans across the Willamette and Columbia rivers in the metro area.

STEFANA YOUNG. *Portland's Little Red Book of Stairs: The City's Ultimate Guide to More Than 150 Curious and Colorful Outdoor Stairways* (1996). A delightful tour of 150 public stairways around the city. Grab a copy of this spiral-bound gem, if you can find one.

► Nonfiction by Portland Authors

GINNY ALLEN AND JODY KLEVIT. *Oregon Painters: The First Hundred Years* (1859–1959). This essential Oregon reference work was produced by two women with more than sixty years of combined experience as docents at the Portland Art Museum. Beautifully illustrated, *Oregon Painters* includes descriptions of more than five hundred artists.

JUDITH BARRINGTON. *Lifesaving: A Memoir* (2000) was nominated for the Pushcart Prize and short-listed for the PEN/Martha Albrand Award for the Art of the Memoir, won the Lambda Literary Award, and was a finalist for the Oregon Book Awards. It followed *Writing the Memoir: From Truth to Art* (1997). Barrington, a native of Brighton, England, who has lived in Portland for three decades, is also an award-winning poet. She received the Stewart H. Holbrook Award for outstanding contributions to Oregon's literary life. Barrington founded Flight of the Mind Writing Workshops and co-founded Soapstone, a Writing Retreat for Women in Oregon. She serves as an online mentor for the University of Minnesota Split Rock program.

JAMES BEARD. *Delights and Prejudices* (1964) was selected for "Literary Oregon, 100 Books, 1800–2000" by the Oregon Cultural Heritage Commission; see "Reading Lists" on page 49). The legendary chef and food writer was a Portland native who briefly attended Reed College. His bounty of cookbooks includes *The James Beard Cookbook* (1970) and *James Beard's Menus for Entertaining* (1965).

PAUL COLLINS. *Banvard's Folly: Thirteen Tales of Renowned Obscurity, Famous Anonymity, and Rotten Luck* (2001); *Not Even Wrong: Adventures in Autism* (2004); *Sixpence House: Lost in a Town of Books* (2003); and *The Trouble with Tom: The Strange Afterlife and Times of Thomas Paine* (2005). Collins edits the Collins Library imprint at McSweeney's Books. Read his compilation of literary oddities at www.collinslibrary.com.

LARRY COLTON. *Counting Coup* (2000); *Goat Brothers* (1993); and *Idol Time: Profile in Blazermania* (1978). Colton, a former pro baseball player and high school English teacher, launched Wordstock, the Portland book festival that debuted in 2005. *Counting Coup*, which was nominated for a Pulitzer Prize, chronicles the struggles of a Crow Indian basketball player named Sharon LaForge. *Goat Brothers* follows the lives of Colton and four of his fraternity brothers at the University of California at Berkeley to middle age. *Idol Time* profiles the Portland Trail Blazers' 1977 championship season.

CHARLES D'AMBROSIO. *Orphans* (2004). From the acclaimed Portland short-story writer who studied with Frank Conroy at the Iowa Writers' Workshop (if you haven't read Conroy's 1967 coming-of-age memoir *Stop-Time*, put this book down *immediately* and run to the library for a copy) comes eleven idiosyncratic essays that should lure you into D'Ambrosio's fiction web. Don't overlook D'Ambrosio's essay, "Seattle, 1974: Writing and Place" in *The Eleventh Draft: Craft and the Writing Life* from the Iowa Writers' Workshop (1999).

BRIAN DOYLE. *The Grail: A Year of Ambling and Shambling through an Oregon Vineyard in Pursuit of the Best Pinot Noir Wine in the Whole Wild World* (2006); *Spirited Men: Story, Soul, and Substance* (2004) ("A Sturdy Man" is my favorite essay); and *The Wet Engine: Exploring the Mad Wild Miracle of the Heart* (2005). Doyle serves as editor of the University of Portland quarterly *Portland Magazine*. He edited *The Best Catholic Writing 2005* and *God Is Love: Essays from Portland Magazine* (2002).

ROCHELL D. ("RO DEEZY") HART. *I Woke Up and Put My Crown On: The Project of 76 Voices* (2005). A native of Portland, Hart spent three years interviewing African-American women nation-wide. The biographies compiled in this volume break down racial stereotypes and generalizations.

KAREN KARBO. *Generation Ex: Tales from the Second Wives' Club* (2001); and *The Stuff of Life: A Daughter's Memoir* (2003). Karbo's nonfiction has appeared in *Vogue, Esquire, The New Republic,* and other national magazines.

ELINOR LANGER. *A Hundred Little Hitlers: The Death of a Black Man, the Trial of a White Racist, and the Rise of the Neo-Nazi Movement in America* (2003); and *Josephine Herbst: The Story She Could Never Tell* (1984). Langer has written for the *New York Review of Books, The New York Times,* and *The Nation.*

JENNIFER LAUCK. *Blackbird: A Childhood Lost and Found* (2000); *Still Waters* (2002); and *Show Me the Way* (2004). *Blackbird* was a *New York Times* bestseller. Her books have been translated into eighteen languages and have been sold in more than twenty countries.

PAUL LINNMAN. *The Exploding Whale: And Other Remarkable Stories from the Evening News* (2003). Linnman, a Portland radio personality who worked as a television reporter and news anchor for thirty years, recounts his legendary 1970 experience at the Oregon coast. Essential reading for all longtime Portlanders.

CHUCK PALAHNIUK. *Stranger Than Fiction: True Stories* (2004). The twenty-three pieces in Palahniuk's first nonfiction collection range from tales about his experiences as an assembly-line worker and hospice volunteer to the violent world of college wrestlers and his father's murder.

JOE SACCO. Pioneer of comics journalism. *Palestine* (2001), originally published as nine-issue comic book and now in its twelfth printing (Fantagraphics, Seattle), won the American Book Award in 1996. Other titles: *But I Like It* (2006); *The Fixer: A Story from Sarajevo* (2003); *Footnotes in Gaza* (2006); *Notes from a Defeatist* (2003); *Safe Area Gorazde: The War in Eastern Bosnia* (2000); and *War's End: Profiles from Bosnia 1995–96* (2005). His work has been published in *Time*, *The New York Times Magazine*, and the *Guardian*. A Malta native and University of Oregon School of Journalism graduate, Sacco lives in Southeast Portland.

KIM STAFFORD. *Early Morning: Remembering My Father, William Stafford* (2002); *Having Everything Right: Essays of Place* (1986); and *The Muses Among Us: Eloquent Listening and Other Pleasures of the Writer's Craft* (2003). Stafford, literary executor of the Estate of William Stafford and founding director of the Northwest Writing Institute at Lewis & Clark College, has worked as an oral historian, letterpress printer, photographer, and teacher.

ANTHONY SWOFFORD. *Jarhead: A Marine's Chronicle of the Gulf War and Other Battles* (2003). Formerly of Portland, Swofford— a University of Iowa Writers' Workshop alum—worked on *Jarhead* at the Sterling Room for Writers at Central Library.

BRENT WALTH. *Fire at Eden's Gate: Tom McCall and the Oregon Story* (1994). One of twelve U.S. journalists selected for the sixty-eighth class of Nieman Fellows at Harvard University in 2005–2006, Walth is a senior reporter for *The Oregonian*. A native of Oregon and winner of a 2001 Pulitzer Prize for public service, Walth enjoys hanging out with his son at Wallace Books in Southeast Portland.

► Fiction by Portland Authors

DIANA ABU-JABER. *Arabian Jazz* (1993) earned the H. L. Davis Award for Fiction at the 1994 Oregon Book Awards. *Crescent* (2003) won the 2004 PEN Center USA Literary Award for Fiction. Abu-Jaber teaches at Portland State University and divides her time between Portland and Miami.

MARC ACITO. *How I Paid for College: A Novel of Sex, Theft, Friendship and Musical Theater* (2004) won the Ken Kesey Award for the Novel at the 2005 Oregon Books Awards. Acito is a New Jersey native who moved to Portland in 1990 after earning a drama degree from Colorado College.

J. CALIFORNIA COOPER. A recent emigrant from Northern California to Portland, Joan California Cooper's work explores the intimate lives and struggles of African-American women. She received the 1989 American Book Award for *Homemade Love*, a collection of short stories, and was named as Black Playwright of the Year in 1978 for *Stars*. Her other honors include the Literary Lion Award and the James Baldwin Writing Award of the American Library Association. She is the author of the novels *Some People, Some Other Place* (2004); *Family: A Novel* (1991); and *In Search of Satisfaction* (1994). Her short-story collections include *The Future Has a Past: Stories* (2000); *The Matter Is Life* (1991); *A Piece of Mine: A New Short Story Collection* (1991); *Some Love, Some Pain, Sometime* (1995); *Some Soul to Keep* (1987); and her first collection as an Oregon author, *Wild Stars Seeking Midnight Suns* (2006).

CHARLES D'AMBROSIO. *The Point and Other Stories* (1995); and *The Dead Fish Museum: Stories* (2006). D'Ambrosio, a Seattle expatriate, has earned the Aga Khan Fiction Prize, the Henfield/Transatlantic Review Award, and a James Michener Fellowship. "The Point" (which originally appeared in *The New Yorker*) earned a place in *Best American Short Stories 1991*, and his first story collection was a *New York Times* Notable Book of the Year and a finalist for the PEN/Hemingway Award. D'Ambrosio's story about rural Oregon, "Jacinta," was published in *Pushcart Prize XIX, Best of the Small Presses, 1994–95*.

MOLLY GLOSS. *The Dazzle of the Day* won the 1998 PEN Center USA Literary Award for Fiction and was a 1997 *New York Times* Notable Book of the Year. *The Jump-Off Creek* (1989) earned the H. L. Davis Award for Fiction at the 1989 Oregon Book Awards and was a PEN/Faulkner Award finalist. *Wild Life* (2000) won the James Tiptree, Jr., Memorial Award for literary fantasy. Gloss grew up in rural Oregon. She has been a frequent instructor at creative writing programs since 1992 and has taught literature of the American West at Portland State University. Be sure to read the author's online essay, "On Becoming a Writer: A Short Autobio-Essay-Thingee," at www.mollygloss.com.

RICHARD HOYT. *Siege* (1987) won the American Mystery Award for best espionage novel. Hoyt, who in 1980 published his first novel, *Decoys: A John Denson Mystery*, is a native of Hermiston, Oregon, and grew up near Umatilla. He is the author of more than twenty mysteries and thrillers, two under the alias of Nicholas van Pelt. He earned a master's degree in journalism from the University of Oregon and a doctorate in American studies from the University of Hawaii. He taught six years at Lewis & Clark College in Portland. *Stomp* is his autobiographical, coming-of-age novel.

KAREN KARBO. *The Diamond Lane* (1991); *Motherhood Made a Man Out of Me* (2000); and *Trespassers Welcome Here* (1989). Each of the three novels was a *New York Times* Notable Book of the Year, and *Trespassers* was a Pulitzer Prize finalist.

URSULA K. LE GUIN. Author of twenty novels, more than a hundred short stories, four collections of essays, six books of poetry, and eleven children's books: Le Guin is a national literary treasure—writer of many forms, including realistic fiction, science fiction, fantasy, children's books, young adults' books, screenplays, essays, criticism, and translations—who has lived in Portland since 1958. Three Le Guin books (including *Searoad: Chronicles of Klatsand*, 1991) have been short-listed for the Pulitzer Prize and American Book Awards. Among her many honors are a National Book Award (*The Farthest Shore*, 1972), five Hugo Awards (including *Buffalo Gals and Other Animal Presences*, 1997), and five Nebula Awards (including *The Left Hand of Darkness*, 1969). Le Guin was named a Science Fiction Writers of America Grand Master and received the Howard Vursell Award from the American Academy of Arts and Letters. Harold Bloom, the Yale University professor and author of *The Western Canon: The Books and School of the Ages*, includes Le Guin among his list of classic American writers. Her contributions to Portland's and Oregon's literary community include participation in Multnomah County Library, Literary Arts, and the Soapstone Foundation.

CRAIG LESLEY. *Storm Riders* (2000) won the H. L. Davis Award for Fiction at the Oregon Book Awards and also earned a Pulitzer Prize nomination. *The Sky Fisherman* (1995) won a Pacific Northwest Booksellers Association Book Award and was nominated for a Pulitzer Prize. *Winterkill* (1984) earned a Pacific Northwest Booksellers Association Book Award. Lesley published his memoir, *Burning Fence: A Western Memoir of Fatherhood* in 2005. He is writer-in-residence at Portland State University.

MILENA McGRAW. *After Dunkirk* (1998). McGraw, who is a librarian at Central Library, grew up in postwar Czechoslovakia and moved to the United States as a young adult. *After Dunkirk* portrays a man coming to terms with life during the Battle of Britain.

WHITNEY OTTO. *How to Make an American Quilt* (1991) was made into a film by Steven Spielberg. Her other fiction includes *A Collection of Beauties at the Height of Their Popularity: A Novel* (2002); *Now You See Her* (1994); and *The Passion Dream Book: A Novel* (1997).

CHUCK PALAHNIUK. Best known for *Fight Club: A Novel* (1996), winner of the H. L. Davis Award for Fiction at the Oregon Book Awards. Other fiction includes *Choke: A Novel* (2001); *Diary: A Novel* (2003); *Haunted: A Novel of Stories* (2005); *Invisible Monsters* (1999); *Lullaby: A Novel* (2002); and *Survivor: A Novel* (1999). I dare him to write a book called *Novel: A Novel*—then again, this isn't the kind of guy you want to get into a game of dare with, so I take it back. (Listen, I even got scared reading his tour book, *Fugitives and Refugees: A Walk in*

Portland, Oregon.) Palahniuk (pronounced *paula-nick*) is a University of Oregon School of Journalism graduate. He divides his time between Oregon and Washington.

JOANNA ROSE. *Little Miss Strange: A Novel* (1997) won the Pacific Northwest Booksellers Association Prize for First Novel and was a finalist for the Oregon Book Awards' H. L. Davis Award for Fiction. Poet and short-story writer as well, Rose was a longtime publicity director for Powell's. She now reviews books for *The Oregonian* and teaches for Dangerous Writing, a community of writers that has formed around Tom Spanbauer.

KEVIN SAMPSELL. *Beautiful Blemish* (2005). Twenty-two stories by the Powell's bookseller, local book reviewer, and editor of *The Insomniac Reader: Stories of the Night* (2005). Sampsell, who runs a micro-press called Future Tense Books, taught creative writing to an eighth grader who now uses the pen name Zoe Trope. He later published the first version of her high school memoir, *Please Don't Kill the Freshman.*

ROBERT SHECKLEY. *Journey Beyond Tomorrow* (1962); and *Dimension of Miracles* (1968). A longtime Portland resident who died in New York in 2005, Sheckley was a science-fiction writer best known for his short stories, such as "The Tenth Victim," which was made into a 1965 film.

TOM SPANBAUER. Works include *Faraway Places* (1988); *In the City of Shy Hunters: A Novel* (2001); and *The Man Who Fell in Love with the Moon: A Novel* (1991). Most recently, Spanbauer published *Now Is the Hour* (2006). He contributed to *Come Home: A Collection of Stories Celebrating the Return to Central Library*

(1997), for which he gets bonus points. Spanbauer teaches Portland workshops called Dangerous Writing, where Chuck Palahniuk and Joanna Rose were his students.

► Poetry by Portland Authors

JAN LEE ANDE. Ande, who holds an interdisciplinary Ph.D. and an MFA in poetry, has taught poetry, ecopoetics, and history of religions since 1993 at Union Institute and University. She authored *Reliquary* (2004) and *Instructions for Walking on Water* (2001); the latter won the 2000 Snyder Prize from Ashland Poetry Press.

LOIS BAKER. *Man Covered with Bees* (2001). Finalist for the Oregon Book Awards Stafford/Hall Award for Poetry.

JUDITH BARRINGTON. *Trying to Be an Honest Woman: Poems* (1985), selected for "Literary Oregon, 100 Books, 1800–2000" by the Oregon Cultural Heritage Commission; *History and Geography: Poems* (1989); and *Horses and the Human Soul: Poems* (2004).

DAVID BIESPIEL. Editor of *Poetry Northwest* and founder of the Attic Writers' Workshop (a literary studio in Portland's Hawthorne District), Biespiel authored *Shattering Air* (1996) and *Wild Civility* (2003). He is a contributor to *American Poetry Review*, *The New Republic*, and *Poetry*. Biespiel has reviewed poetry for *The New York Times*, and he writes a monthly column about poetry for *The Oregonian*. He was awarded a Stegner Fellowship in Poetry at Stanford University and a National Endowment for the Arts literature fellowship. He teaches at Oregon State University and Portland State University.

KAREN BRAUCHER. *Sending Messages over Inconceivable Distances* (2000). Finalist for the Oregon Book Awards Stafford/Hall Award for Poetry.

TOM BREMER. *Just Once: Poems* (2001). Finalist for the Oregon Book Awards Stafford/Hall Award for Poetry.

HENRY CARLILE. *Rain: Poems* (1994); *The Rough-Hewn Table: Poems* (1971); and *Running Lights* (1981). *Rain* was a finalist for the Oregon Book Awards Stafford/Hall Award for Poetry.

WALT CURTIS. *Peckerneck Country: The Selected Poems of Walt Curtis* (1978); and *Rhymes for Alice Bluelight* (1984). Curtis has authored many books, including *Mala Noche*, on which Portland director Gus Van Sant based his first feature film in 1985. For three decades, Curtis has co-hosted "The Talking Earth," a poetry program that airs Mondays, 10 p.m.–11 p.m., on nonprofit radio station KBOO (90.7 FM, Portland).

MICHELE GLAZER. *It Is Hard to Look at What We Came to Think We'd Come to See* (1997), winner, Associated Writing Programs' award series in poetry; and *Aggregate of Disturbances: Poems* (2004), Iowa Poetry Prize. Her work has been published in *The Harvard Review* and *Ploughshares*, among other journals and anthologies. Glazer, who attended Portland's Catlin Gable High School, is an associate professor of English at Portland State University. She earned an MFA from the Iowa Writers' Workshop. It's a treat to hear her read in person.

JAMES GRABILL. *An Indigo Scent after the Rain* (2003) and *Listening to the Leaves Form: Poems* (1997) were Oregon Book Awards finalists. *Poem Rising out of the Earth and Standing up in Someone* (1994) won the Stafford/Hall Award for Poetry.

KATHLEEN HALME. *Equipoise* (1998); *The Everlasting Universe of Things* (1994); and *Every Substance Clothed: Poems* (1995). Halme is married to Alan Cordle, the Portland Community College reference librarian who publishes the poetry watchdog Web site "Foetry" at www.foetry.com.

JERRY HARP. Co-editor of *A Poetry Criticism Reader* (2006), Harp has published *Gatherings* (2005) and *Creature* (2003). He teaches at Lewis & Clark College.

ROCHELL D. ("RO DEEZY") HART. *A Black Girl's Song* (2001). Hart became the first African-American woman from Oregon to appear at the National Poetry Slam in 1999. *A Black Girl's Song* earned an Oregon Book Awards nomination. She has also recorded a CD titled *PIMP: Poetic Intellectual Making Progress*.

JUDITH MONTGOMERY. *Passion: Poems*. Winner of the Oregon Book Awards Stafford/Hall Award for Poetry in 2000.

PAULANN PETERSEN. *The Animal Bride: Poems* (1994); *Blood Silk: Poems* (2003); *Under the Sign of a Neon Wolf* (1989); and *The Wild Awake: A Reading from the Erotic Compass of the World* (2002). A former Stegner Fellow at Stanford University and the recipient of two Carolyn Kizer Awards, Peterson has published poems in the Poetry in Motion series aboard buses and MAX Light Rail.

CARLOS REYES. The longtime editor and publisher of Trask House Books in Portland, Reyes has authored many chapbooks and collections, including *At the Edge of the Western Wave: Poems* (2004) and

Nightmarks (1990). *A Suitcase Full of Crows: Poems* (1995) won the Bluestem Poetry Award and was an Oregon Book Awards finalist.

VERN RUTSALA. *The Moment's Equation* (2004). Rutsala was the 2005 National Book Award finalist for poetry and the first Oregon poet nominated since William Stafford won in 1963. He retired in 2004 after more than four decades of teaching at Lewis & Clark College. Other works include *A Handbook for Writers: New and Selected Prose Poems* (2004); *The Journey Begins* (1976); *Laments* (1975); *Little-Known Sports* (1994); *The New Life* (1978); *Paragraphs* (1978); *Ruined Cities: Poems* (1987); *Selected Poems* (1991); *Walking Home from the Icehouse: Poems* (1981); and *The Window: Poems* (1964).

WILLA SCHNEBERG. *Box Poems* (1979); *In the Margins of the World*, which won the Oregon Book Awards Stafford/Hall Award for Poetry in 2002.

SAMUEL L. SIMPSON. *The Gold-Gated West: Songs and Poems* (1910). "Beautiful Willamette," the most famous poem by Oregon's first poet laureate, was originally published in the *Albany Democrat* newspaper of April 18, 1868. Simpson, who graduated with a law degree from Willamette University and became a journalist and editor, is buried at Portland's Lone Fir Cemetery, 2115 SE Morrison St.

KIM STAFFORD. *Braided Apart: Poems* (1976); *The Granary: Poems* (1982); *A Gypsy's History of the World* (1976); and *A Thousand Friends of Rain: New and Selected Poems, 1976–1998* (1999). Stafford is founding director of the Northwest Writing Institute at Lewis & Clark College's Graduate School of Education. He serves as literary executor for the estate of his father, William Stafford. He has authored a dozen books of poetry and prose.

WILLIAM STAFFORD. A native of Kansas who taught at Lewis & Clark College for more than three decades, Stafford won the National Book Award in 1963 for *Traveling through the Dark* (1962), which was also selected for "Literary Oregon, 100 Books, 1800–2000" by the Oregon Cultural Heritage Commission. He served as Poetry Consultant for the Library of Congress in 1970–1971. Governor Tom McCall appointed Stafford as Oregon Poet Laureate in 1975. The author of sixty-seven volumes, Stafford published his first book, *West of Your City*, at age forty-six in 1960. Graywolf Press published *The Way It Is: New and Selected Poems* in 1998. The Friends of William Stafford maintains an online bibliography, selected Stafford poems, audio samples, and video samples at www.williamstafford.org.

LISA STEINMAN. Steinman, who has taught at Reed College since 1976, has published four books of poetry, a chapbook, and two books about poetry. *Carslaw's Sequences: Poems* (2003) and *Ordinary Songs* (1996) were Oregon Book Awards finalists. *A Book of Other Days* (1993) earned the Stafford/Hall Award. She won a National Endowment for the Humanities fellowship in 2005 and is researching and writing a book on American poetry from the 1950s through the present.

PRIMUS ST. JOHN. *Communion: Poems, 1976–1998* (1999), winner of the Western States Book Award; *Dreamer: Poems* (1990), winner of the Oregon Book Awards Hazel Hall Award for Poetry; *Love Is Not a Consolation: It Is a Light* (1982); and *Skins on the Earth* (1976). A Portland State University professor for more than thirty years, St. John is co-editor of *From Here We Speak: An Anthology of Oregon Poetry* (1993) and a co-compiler of the children's book *Zero Makes*

Me Hungry: A Collection of Poems for Today (1976). His work has appeared in numerous journals and anthologies. Born in New York City, St. John attended the University of Maryland and Lewis & Clark College. He worked with the National Endowment for the Arts to launch the Poets in the Schools program.

SANDRA STONE. *Cocktails with Brueghel at the Museum Cafe* (1997) won the Oregon Book Awards Hazel Hall Award. Bibliophiles will enjoy her poem "My Artifacts, My Children, My Parents, My Books, My Continent, My Pond; Hokusai, Paint-Crazy Old Man."

MARY SZYBIST. *Granted* (2003), Szybist's first collection of poetry, was a finalist for the National Book Critics Circle Award. A graduate of the University of Iowa Writers' Workshop, she teaches at Lewis & Clark College.

► Children's Literature by Portland Authors

CARMEN T. BERNIER-GRAND. *Cesar: Si, Se Puede! = Yes, We Can!* A tribute to Cesar Chávez in poems, this American Library Association Notable Book is illustrated by Caldecott medalist David Diaz.

BEVERLY CLEARY. *Dear Mr. Henshaw* (1983) won the John Newberry Medal. Two Newberry Honor Books are *Ramona and Her Father* (1978) and *Ramona Quimby, Age 8* (1982). Her memoirs include *A Girl From Yamhill* (1988) and *My Own Two Feet* (1995). Cleary is recipient of thirty-five state awards based on the votes of young readers and winner of the American Library Association Laura Ingalls Wilder Award (1975), the Catholic Library Association Regina Medal Award (1980), the University of Southern Mississippi Silver Medallion (1982), and the Children's Book Council Everychild Award (1985). The Library of Congress named her a Living Legend in 2000. Cleary's books have been published in twenty countries and in fourteen languages. See the signed foreign-language editions, donated by the author, at Central Library. Cleary is a native of McMinnville, Oregon, and she attended Fernwood and Gregory Heights grammar schools and Grant High School in Portland. Visit the Beverly Cleary Sculpture Garden at Grant Park (see "Hollywood Library"). And visit "The World of Beverly Cleary" at www.beverlycleary.com.

NANCY COFFELT. *The Dog Who Cried Woof* (1995); *Dogs in Space: The Great Space Doghouse* (2001, also available in Spanish); *Good Night, Sigmund* (1992); *Tom's Fish* (1994); and *What's Cookin'? A Happy Birthday Counting Book* (2003). Coffelt is also an illustrator.

SUSAN FLETCHER. *Alphabet of Dreams* (1996); *Dragon's Milk* (1992); *Flight of the Dragon Kyn* (1993); *Shadow Spinner* (1998); *Sign of the Dove* (1996); and *Walk Across the Sea* (2001). Fletcher holds an M.A. in English and is on leave from Vermont College, where she has taught in its Writing for Children program.

DAVID GIFALDI. *Ben, King of the River* (2001); *The Boy Who Spoke Colors* (1993); *Rearranging and Other Stories* (1998); and *Toby Scudder, Ultimate Warrior* (1993). Gifaldi, author of seven books, lives in Portland and teaches in the Vancouver School District.

PAMELA SMITH HILL. *A Voice from the Border* (1998) won the Oregon Book Awards Leslie Bradshaw Award. Hill also authored *Ghost Horses* (1999) and *The Last Grail Keeper* (2001).

KAREN KARBO. *Minerva Clark Gets a Clue* (2005). In Karbo's first book for young readers, an electrified thirteen-year-old sleuth probes the mysterious death of a bookstore clerk.

ERIC A. KIMMEL. Formerly a Portland State University education professor, Kimmel has authored more than fifty children's books, including *Hershel and the Hanukkah Goblins* (1990 Caldecott Honor Book), *Wonders and Miracles* (2004 National Jewish Book Award for books for children), and *I Took My Frog to the Library* (1990). Watch for *Stormy's Hat* in September 2007. The Oregon Reading Association honored Kimmel with the Ulrich H. Hardt Award for his contributions to reading literacy. Free, downloadable teacher's guides to eleven of Kimmel's books are available at his Web site: www.ericakimmel.com.

MICHELLE ROEHM McCANN. *Boys Who Rocked the World* (2001); *Finding Fairies: Secrets for Attracting Little People from Around the World* (2001); *Girls Who Rocked the World* (1998); *Going Places: True Tales from Young Travelers* (2003); and *Luba: The Angel of Bergen-Belsen* (2003). McCann, who grew up just off Klickitat Street in Ramona Quimby's neighborhood, teaches children's literature at Portland State University. Luba won the Eloise Jarvis McGraw Award for Children's Literature at the 2004 Oregon Book Awards and earned a nomination for the American Library Association's prestigious "Best Books for Young Adults" list.

ELOISE McGRAW. McGraw authored more than two dozen books and was a three-time Newberry Honor winner: *Moccasin Trail* (1953); *The Golden Goblet* (1962); and *The Moorchild* (1997).

McGraw was in fairly good company in 1953—another of the Newberry Honor Books that year was E. B. White's *Charlotte's Web*. McGraw won the Oregon Book Awards Leslie Bradshaw Award for Young Readers for *The Striped Ships* (1992) and *The Moorchild*. McGraw's *A Really Weird Summer* won the 1977 Edgar Allen Poe Award for best juvenile mystery. Online treasure: Listen to the 1983 recording of McGraw talking about the reader–writer relationship, available at the Hungry Tiger Press Web site, www.hungrytigerpress.com/tigertreats/mcgraw.shtml.

SARA RYAN. *The Empress of the World* (2002 Oregon Book Awards Leslie Bradshaw Award for Young Readers). Ryan is a Teen Services specialist at Multnomah County Library.

GRAHAM SALISBURY. Three-time winner of Oregon Book Awards Leslie Bradshaw Award for Young Readers: *Blue Skin of the Sea* (1993); *Shark Bait* (1998); and *Under the Blood Red Sun* (1995). *Blue Skin of the Sea* also won the PEN/Norma Klein Award, while *Under the Blood Red Sun* earned the Scott O'Dell Award for Historical Fiction. Recent works: *House of the Red Fish* (2006) and *Eyes of the Emperor* (2005).

ALEXANDER SCHARBACH. *Matthew Calbraith Perry: Boy Sailor* (1955); and *The Gold Race* (1956). Scharbach was a native of Gervais, Oregon, who taught English at Portland State University from 1952 until his retirement in 1974. (I grew up with *Boy Sailor* and a dozen other orange-covered volumes from the Bobbs-Merrill Childhood of Famous Americans series on the shelf of my bedroom bookcase, which was really a secret door to the attic.)

DAVID MICHAEL SLATER. *Cheese Louise!* (1999); *Jacques and Spock* (2004); and *The Ring Bear: A Rascally Wedding Adventure* (2004). A thirty-six-year-old native of Pittsburgh, Slater teaches seventh-grade language arts in Beaverton, Oregon.

➤ Reading Lists

LITERARY OREGON, ONE HUNDRED BOOKS, 1800–2000
Oregon Cultural Heritage Commission
P.O. Box 3588, 97208
503-285-8279
encanto@ochcom.org
www.ochcom.org/100books

NOVELS SET IN PORTLAND
Multnomah County Library (Web site only)
Reference Line, 503-998-5234
www.multcolib.org/books/lists/portlandsetting.html

OREGON AUTHORS
Oregon Library Association
P.O. Box 2042, Salem, 97308
503-370-7019
ola@olaweb.org
www.olaweb.org

➤ Portland Literary Periodicals

BURNSIDE REVIEW

An independent, nonprofit poetry journal founded in 2004 by editor Sid Miller, a Pushcart Prize nominee in 2004, whose chapbook

Quietly Waiting was published by White Heron Press. *Burnside Review* is published twice yearly, February and August. Single issue: $6. One-year subscription: $10.

P.O. Box 1782, 97207
sid@burnsidereview.org
burnsidereview.org

ELLIPSIS MAGAZINE

Founded in 2005, *Ellipsis* publishes original fiction in serial installments. The magazine focuses on literature in cinema, television, and music through interviews and articles with writers and artists. Published ten times per year. Single issue: $7.95. One-year subscription: $50.

P.O. Box 86829, 97286
503-233-4093
editors@waywardcouch.com
www.waywardcouch.com

EYE~RHYME: JOURNAL OF NEW LITERATURE

Pinball Publishing, an independent literary press in Southeast Portland, produced the first issue of *eye~rhyme*, which includes contemporary fiction and poetry, in the summer of 1999. Local readers will appreciate Issue 7, "Roses Are Red," an all-Portland issue that includes short fiction, poetry, interviews, and artwork from City of Roses residents.

Pinball Publishing
1003 SE Grant St., 97214
info@pinballpublishing.com
www.eye-rhyme.com

GLIMMER TRAIN STORIES

Short-story quarterly founded in 1990 by sisters Susan Burmeister-Brown and Linda Swanson-Davies. Each issue publishes eight to twelve new stories by established writers and newcomers. Includes interviews. Single issue: $12. One-year subscription (four issues): $36. Two-year subscription: $58.

1211 NW Glisan St., Suite 207, 97209
503-221-0836
eds@glimmertrain.com
www.glimmertrain.com

GOBSHITE QUARTERLY: YOUR ROSETTA STONE FOR THE NEW WORLD ORDER

Edited by R. V. Branham, *GobQ* encompasses world politics and literature. The first issue in February 2003 included a cast as diverse as Karel Capek and Chuck Palahniuk. Find out how the quarterly enlisted its name under "Gobwords" at the quarterly's Web site. Single issue: $7. One-year subscription: $20.

P.O. Box 11346, 97211-0346
www.gobshitequarterly.com

THE GROVE REVIEW: A LITERARY JOURNAL

Published twice yearly by The Grove Review, Inc., a nonprofit, beginning with a fall/winter issue in 2004. Matt Barry, editor and publisher. Contributors have included Ursula K. Le Guin and Kim Stafford. Single issue: $11. One-year subscription: $20.

PMB 137, 1631 NE Broadway, 97232
editor@thegrovereview.org
www.thegrovereview.org

OPEN SPACES: VIEWS FROM THE NORTHWEST

Founded in 1997, *Open Spaces* is published quarterly and includes short stories, essays, and poetry in addition to its nonfiction features that explore issues in the environment, healthcare, public policy, and international affairs. Distributed nationwide. Single issue: $7.95. One-year subscription: $25.

PMB 134, 6327-C SW Capitol Highway, 97239
503-227-3401
info@open-spaces.com
www.open-spaces.com

POETRY NORTHWEST

In an effort to bridge the worlds of public and academic poetry and prose as well as other arts, The Attic Writers' Workshop in Portland revived publication of the nonprofit *Poetry Northwest* in May 2006. The University of Washington published the original journal, which was the longest-running poetry-only periodical in the country, from 1959 to 2002. Now edited by Portland poet and critic David Biespiel, the new *Poetry Northwest* is published in a magazine format that features poetry and prose. Single issue: $7.95. One-year subscription: $15. Two-year subscription: $25. Lifetime subscription: $400.

4232 SE Hawthorne Blvd., 97215
503-236-0615
editors@poetrynw.org
www.poetrynw.org

THE PORTLAND REVIEW LITERARY JOURNAL

Published by Portland State University since 1956, *The Portland Review Literary Journal* features short fiction, poetry, and art. This journal is published three times per year. One-year subscription costs $28. Individual issues can be purchased for $8 at the PSU Bookstore and several downtown area bookstores—see the Web site for a complete list.

P.O. Box 347, 97207-0347
503-725-4533
ncj@pdx.edu
www.portlandreview.org

TIN HOUSE MAGAZINE

Founded by Win McCormack. First issue in May 1999 included fiction by David Foster Wallace and nonfiction by

Rick Moody. Subsequent contributors have included Amy Hempl (Issue 3), Richard Ford (Issue 9), Jonathan Lethem (Issues 10 and 14), and Portland's Charles D'Ambrosio (Issue 19). $19.95 per year (four issues).

P.O. Box 10500, 97210.
1-800-786-3424
info@tinhouse.com
www.tinhouse.com

2 GYRLZ QUARTERLY

Published by the nonprofit 2 Gyrlz Performative Arts, this literary/arts journal publishes fiction, poetry, and articles in limited, hand-bound editions with silkscreened/letterpressed covers. Individual issues are $11.

3439 NE Sandy, #513, 97232
2006@2GQ.org
www.2GQ.org

PART THREE

Act Locally: Participate and Volunteer

EACH OF US IN THIS City of Readers has our own story about how we fell in love with reading and books. For Michael Powell, the man who runs the biggest independent bookstore on earth, a formative influence was Flora E. Robison, the librarian at Rose City Park Elementary School in Northeast Portland, who enlisted the young Powell's help to distribute books that his schoolmates had purchased from Scholastic Press.

Each of our stories has a number of chapters, because reading is a pursuit that changes as we mature and leads to unexpected discoveries. In the course of researching this book, I talked with John

Henley—the novelist, Portland State University bookselling instructor, and Great Northwest Bookstore manager—who brought Ernest Haycox's 1946 *Long Storm* to my attention when I asked him about novels set in Portland. And there was Susan Smallreed, the children's librarian at the Multnomah County Library Northwest Branch, who unfurled a scroll of Portland children's authors and illustrators for me. These are the kinds of people whose generosity of time and spirit keeps our love affair with books fresh and exciting, and it is incumbent on each of us to share our passion for reading with others: family, friends, co-workers, and children.

There are so many ways to participate in the community of readers. Find one or several that you enjoy. Note: the following selections do not include resources that are primarily writing-focused (unless they are literacy-focused). To add to the reading or book-related resource list, please post a note at the *City of Readers* forum at www.cityofreaders.com.

► Classes

PORTLAND COMMUNITY COLLEGE

If you're looking for an opportunity to meet and study with other readers, consider the wealth of resources available at Portland Community College, including credit classes such as "Introduction to Children's Literature," "Images of Women in Literature," "African-American Literature," and "The Bible as Literature." Noncredit options abound, too: PCC's Community Education program offers classes just for personal enrichment (think "no grades or tests") and invites you to suggest, or even teach, a class yourself. These are held at PCC campuses and many neighborhood locations around the city. Tuition is low, although you'll pay more for credit.

12000 SW 49th Ave., 97219
503-244-6111
www.pcc.edu (credit classes); www.pcc.edu/communityed
(noncredit classes)

PORTLAND STATE UNIVERSITY EXTENDED STUDIES, INSTITUTE OF READING DEVELOPMENT, SUMMER READING SKILLS PROGRAMS

Portland State University Extended Studies department holds monthlong summer reading skills programs for all ages in phonics, comprehension, vocabulary, study skills, and speed reading. These are offered in conjunction with the Institute of Reading Development, a private reading school. All programs meet once a week on campus.

1825 SW Broadway, 97207
1-800-978-3532
admission@pdx.edu
www.pdx.edu

▶ Events

There's a frenzy of reading activity in Portland year-round. In addition to the usual slew of author appearances, library lectures and exhibitions, and volunteers working throughout the city, annual happenings can carve *entire days* out of a book lover's calendar. In fact, the scale, quality, and diversity of these events point to the emergence of Portland as a nationwide center for literary arts. I'm reluctant to make the suggestion, but *put down your book* and join the fray!

EVERYBODY READS

Reading the same book at roughly the same time as fifty thousand or so people really gives you quite a few opportunities for conversation. Since 2003, thousands of teens and adults in the Portland metro area have participated in Everybody Reads during January and February. You can catch up with Portland's ongoing literary conversation by reading the first four Everybody Reads books: *A Lesson Before Dying* by Ernest J. Gaines; *Fahrenheit 451* by Ray Bradbury; *The House on Mango Street* by Sandra Cisneros; and *The Kite Runner* by Khaled Hosseini. Everybody Reads is funded by The Library Foundation and coordinated by Multnomah County Library.

The Library Foundation, 522 SW 5th Ave., Suite 1103, 97204
503-223-4008
information@libraryfoundation.org
www.multcolib.org/reads

FRIENDS OF THE LIBRARY USED BOOK SALE

Among used-book deal-seekers in Oregon, this annual fall sale is the equivalent of Black Friday, that warm-and-fuzzy first day of the holiday shopping season when typically nonathletic consumers adopt the aggressiveness of roller-derby skaters as they elbow their way to sale tables. Really, the lion's share of shoppers at this four-day event are well-mannered bibliophiles—as opposed to the scouts who tear through the tables at the members-only sale with cell phones, scanning bar codes and tossing books into boxes.

In October 2005, Friends of the Library hosted its thirty-second annual and raised more than $93,000 for Multnomah County Library. There's a huge selection of hardcovers and large paperbacks, pocket-sized paperbacks, audiotapes, CDs, DVDs, LPs, maps, pamphlets, sheet music, and videos. Prices generally range from $1.50 for hardcovers and large paperbacks to 50 cents for pocket-sized paperbacks. Volumes with dots on their spines are priced as marked. Other materials range from 25 cents to $4. Friends of the Library members (individual annual dues $30) shop earliest. Cash, checks, Visa, and MasterCard. Donate books and other materials year-round at any library branch.

522 SW 5th Ave., Suite 1103, 97204
503-224-9176
foladmin@europa.com
www.friends-library.org

OREGON BOOK AWARDS

Oregon Book Awards will mark its twentieth anniversary in November 2006. Categories include poetry, novel, short fiction, general nonfiction, creative nonfiction, drama, children's literature, and young-adult literature. During the past nineteen years, Literary Arts, which sponsors the Oregon Book Awards, has honored four hundred Oregon writers and publishers and has distributed $450,000 in fellowships and awards. Oregon Book Awards Authors Tour gives finalists an opportunity to present their work in libraries and bookstores statewide.

Literary Arts, 224 NW 13th Ave., Suite 306, 97209
503-227-2583
la@literary-arts.org
www.literary-arts.org

POETRY DOWNTOWN

Annual series of three to four poets in early spring. In 2005, U.S. Poet Laureate Ted Kooser appeared, as well as W. S. Merwin and Maxine Kumin. Tickets discounted for students and seniors.

Literary Arts, 224 NW 13th Ave., Suite 306, 97209
503-227-2583
la@literary-arts.org
www.literary-arts.org

PORTLAND ARTS AND LECTURES

One of the best-attended lecture series nationwide, Portland Arts and Lectures debuted in 1984. The lectures, which begin in September and run through April, are a program of Literary Arts, a statewide nonprofit. The series features six leading figures in literature and the arts who talk about their work and today's philosophical issues. Past speakers who took the stage at Arlene Schnitzer Concert Hall have included the novelist, critic, and short-story writer Cynthia Ozick; Alexander McCall Smith, author of *The No. 1 Ladies' Detective Agency* mysteries; Marilynne Robinson, winner of the 2005 Pulitzer Prize for fiction (*Gilead*); David Sedaris; and Simon Winchester. General admission for the full series costs $115; partial series packages are available. Patron tickets (post-lecture receptions with speakers) and reserved seating are available. General-admission tickets for individual events go on sale in mid-August.

Literary Arts, 224 NW 13th Ave., Suite 306, 97209
503-227-2583
la@literary-arts.org
www.literary-arts.org

PORTLAND ZINE SYMPOSIUM

First held in July 2001, this three-day summer conference and social at Portland State University's Smith Memorial Student Union explores underground publishing and the do-it-yourself (DIY) culture. The sixth annual Portland Zine Symposium was held in August 2006. Admission is free.

P.O. Box 5901, 97228-5901
pdxzinesymposium@riseup.net
www.pdxzines.com

STUMPTOWN COMICS FEST

This fall festival is focused on comics creators. Events include signings, presentations, panel discussions, and films. The inaugural event in 2004 featured twenty-two exhibitors and drew 150 comics fans to The Old Church in downtown Portland. The 2005 show, held at Portland State University's Smith Memorial Ballroom, showcased eighty West Coast exhibitors and drew attendance of five hundred. Admission in 2005 was $3.

www.pdxcomix.com

SUMMER READING, MULTNOMAH COUNTY LIBRARY

Support from The Library Foundation has helped Summer Reading grow tenfold. More than fifty thousand children and teens, from birth to age eighteen, now participate in this Multnomah County Library program. Summer Reading helps children retain or improve reading skills that can be lost when school is not in session. The program encourages children to set goals, choose books, and reach reading milestones with the help of parents, library staff, or volunteers.

503-988-5402
www.multcolib.org/summer

TEEN READ MONTH, MULTNOMAH COUNTY LIBRARY

The fourth-annual Teen Author Lecture in October 2005 was delivered by Garth Nix, award-winning Australian author of

Sabriel, *Lirael*, *Abhorsen*, *Shade's Children*, and the *Keys to the Kingdom* series. Teen Read Month also offers young patrons a chance to reduce library fines and earn bookstore discount coupons.

503-988-5402
www.multcolib.org/feature/teenreadmonth.html

TIN HOUSE SUMMER WRITERS WORKSHOP READINGS

In the outdoor amphitheater that overlooks the Reed College canyon: a week of July evening readings by prominent American writers of fiction, nonfiction, and poetry who are faculty and guests of the Tin House Summer Writers Workshop. The 2005 lineup included Francine Prose, whose novel *Blue Angel* was nominated for the National Book Award in 2000, and Portland's Charles D'Ambrosio (author of *The Point and Other Stories* and *The Dead Fish Museum: Stories*). Cost is $75.

503-219-0622
tinhouse@pcspublink.com
www.tinhouse.com

WORDSTOCK

Wordstock has yet to gain the fame of its 1969 namesake, but Portland author Larry Colton (*Counting Coup* and *Goat Brothers*) has this literary jam session well on its way. The festival's inaugural year in April 2005 attracted more than 35,000 attendees over six days of events, including a weekend book fair at the Oregon Convention Center, where there was a two-day downpour of readings, workshops, exhibits, and panel discussions. More than two hundred authors—including Norman Mailer, John Irving, Ursula K. Le Guin, Sarah Vowell, Judith Barrington, and Jean Auel—took to the stage. Attendees mixed with authors and browsed among the booths of independent presses, literary journals, marketing and editorial services, agents, and nonprofit organizations. Workshops included topics such as screenwriting and finding an agent. Admission to the exhibit hall in 2006 was $3, while tickets for special events ranged higher. Proceeds benefit Community of Writers, a Portland nonprofit organization dedicated to bringing writing resources to local schools.

1500 SW 12th Ave., 97201
503-546-1013
www.wordstockfestival.com

ZINESTERS TALKING

This free monthly program of Multnomah County Library gives local zinesters a forum to read from their works and sell their zines. Typically held weeknights at branches. See Web site for schedule. Check out the library's excellent online guide to zines at www.multcolib.org/books/zines/index.html, which includes zine history and places to find zines in Portland.

Multnomah County Library Administration
205 NE Russell St., 97212-3796

503-988-5402
zines@multcolib.org
www.multcolib.org/events/zinesters.html

► Organizations

FRIENDS OF MYSTERY

A nonprofit educational and literary organization for Portland mystery readers and writers. The Bloody Thursday lecture series, featuring authors, law enforcement officers, and criminologists takes place on the fourth Thursday of January, March, May, and September and the third Thursday of November. Meets at 7 p.m., Legacy Good Samaritan Medical Center auditorium, 1040 NW 22nd Ave. (at Marshall Street). Free parking in hospital structures. Each spring, a volunteer committee announces an annual award called The Spotted Owl for the best mystery by a writer from the Pacific Northwest (including Alaska, Idaho, Oregon, Washington, and British Columbia). Publishes a bimonthly newsletter, *The Blood-Letter*, including events, book reviews, and interviews. The Friends of Mystery reading group (see "Reading Communities" in "Act Locally") meets the third Wednesday of every month. Thursday events and reading group are free. To become a member, annual dues are $20.

P.O. Box 8251, 97207
503-241-0759
info@friendsofmystery.org
www.friendsofmystery.org

FRIENDS OF THE LIBRARY

Founded in 1972, this nonprofit organization is dedicated to serving Multnomah County Library by promoting public involvement in the library and by raising money through membership fees, the Friends' Library Store, and the sales of used books (see "Events" in part three, "Act Locally"). The annual meeting in May 2005 featured Whitney Otto, Portland author of the bestselling *How to Make an American Quilt* and *A Collection of Beauties at the Height of Their Popularity*.

522 SW 5th Ave., 97209
503-224-9176
foladmin@europa.com
www.friends-library.org

INDEPENDENT PUBLISHING RESOURCE CENTER

Freedom of expression has an advocate in the Independent Publishing Resource Center. The IPRC is an extraordinary opportunity for Portlanders who want to produce and distribute publications at affordable prices. Resources include knowledgeable, helpful volunteers; a library of more than 5,300 zines (see "Private" in part five, "Borrow Locally"), Internet access for research and networking; workspaces and tools for the production of small pamphlets, booklets, and hand-bound books; a copier and tabletop letterpresses for small print runs; a graphics computer workstation for word processing and layout; fax and phone. Annual membership, on a sliding scale, costs $45-$100. Nonmember rate is $5 per hour. Orientation sessions are held the second Tuesday of each month from 7 p.m. to 8 p.m.

917 SW Oak St., Suite 218, 97205
503-827-0249
info@iprc.org
www.iprc.org

THE LIBRARY FOUNDATION

This nonprofit, founded in 1995 at the time of the Central Library renovation, has raised $20 million from nine thousand donors to support Multnomah County Library programs, collections, and buildings. Its current focus is on literacy programs such as Summer Reading, which drew participation from fifty thousand children in 2005. Publishes a newsletter, *Gateways*; back issues available on its Web site.

522 SW 5th Ave., Suite 1103, 97204
503-223-4008
information@libraryfoundation.org
www.libraryfoundation.org

LITERARY ARTS

This Portland-based nonprofit delivers seven programs. "Delve: Readers' Seminars," the newest Literary Arts program, offers informal readers' seminars focused on a great book and led by a local scholar. The Oregon Book Awards—founded in 1993 by

Portland literary advocate Brian Booth as a program of the Oregon Institute of Literary Arts—are held each November and present prizes to state residents for poetry, fiction, literary nonfiction, drama, and young readers' literature. Oregon Literary Fellowships, which have awarded a half-million dollars to nearly five hundred writers since 1987, support emerging writers and small independent publishers statewide. Portland Arts and Lectures features an annual series of six leading authors, historians, artists, and critics. Poetry Downtown brings acclaimed poets to town for readings and discussions. Poetry in Motion graces TriMet buses and trains with verse. Writers in the Schools places Oregon authors for semester-long residencies in Portland public high schools.

224 NW 13th Ave., Suite 306, 97209
503-227-2583
la@literary-arts.org
www.literary-arts.org

OREGON ARTS COMMISSION

Founded in 1967, the Oregon Arts Commission is funded by the state and the National Endowment for the Arts and fosters the arts statewide. Programs include "Poetry Out Loud," a national initiative that involves students in the study and public recitation of classic poetry.

775 Summer St. NE, Suite 200, Salem, 97301
503-986-0082
oregon.artscomm@state.or.us
www.oregonartscommission.org/main.php

OREGON COUNCIL FOR THE HUMANITIES

The Oregon Council for the Humanities is a nonprofit, independent affiliate of the National Endowment for the Humanities. The council's outstanding *Oregon Humanities* magazine is free. Recent issues have focused on marriage, pop culture, and belief. The council also publishes *Verso*, an online publication for high school and college students that presents topics central to young people in their roles as emerging citizens. Visit www.versomagazine.org.

812 SW Washington St., Suite 225, 97205
503-241-0543
och@oregonhum.org
www.oregonhum.org

OREGON CULTURAL HERITAGE COMMISSION

Concerned that arts organizations were focusing only on contemporary literary authors, Brian Booth co-founded the Oregon Cultural Heritage Commission (OCHC) in 1991 to promote the state's literary and cultural heritage. Booth, who practices law in Portland, is a devoted scholar of and advocate for the state's literary heritage. Of keen interest are the OCHC "Profiles of Oregon Originals" online biographies of nearly thirty creative figures, including James Beard, Louise Bryant, Ernest Haycox, Elizabeth Henley, Joaquin Miller, Opal Whiteley, and C.E.S. Wood. In celebration of the Oregon State Library's centennial, the commission chose one hundred books from the years 1800 to 2000 that exemplify the best of Oregon's rich literary heritage. The exhibit can be viewed from

8 a.m. to 5 p.m., Monday through Friday, on the second floor of the State Library, 250 Winter St. NE, Salem. A list of the books, "Literary Oregon: One Hundred Books, 1800–2000," is available on the OCHC Web site. The commission also has published the "Writers of West Portland" map, available in print and online at www.ochcom.org/writersmap, which shows residences and working addresses of nearly thirty prominent Portland writers through 1970, including Ursula K. Le Guin, Katherine Dunn, and Ken Kesey.

P.O. Box 3588, 97208
503-285-8279 or 503-292-6439
encanto@ochcom.org
www.ochcom.org

OREGON CULTURAL TRUST

Formed in 1999, the Oregon Cultural Trust raises funds to invest in Oregon's arts, humanities, and heritage. Oregon offers a unique tax credit for the support of the trust. Make a gift to one of more than a thousand qualifying nonprofit organizations and a matching gift to the Oregon Cultural Trust to claim a tax credit and support culture in Oregon.

775 Summer St. NE, Suite 200, Salem, 97301
503-986-0088
cultural.trust@state.or.us
www.culturaltrust.org

REGIONAL ARTS AND CULTURE COUNCIL

Founded in 1995, the Regional Arts and Culture Council works to integrate arts and culture in all aspects of public life. The newsletter *Art Notes* is one of the most comprehensive listings in the Northwest of opportunities for artists and cultural organizations, including notices of literary grants and fellowships, competitions, jobs, workshops, supplies, and services that the community can use.

108 NW 9th Ave., Suite 300, 97209-3318
503-823-5111
info@racc.org
www.racc.org

STREET ROOTS

This nonprofit organization founded in 1998 publishes the *street roots* newspaper, which is printed twice monthly and serves as an advocate for Portland's homeless. An outstanding feature of *street roots* is its "Rose City Resource" list of services for people experiencing homelessness and poverty. Certified vendors, who are homeless, purchase papers for 30 cents each and sell them for $1. The organization supports a weekly writers' group that encourages homeless and low-income individuals, many of whom also are vendors, to publish in the newspaper.

211 NW Davis St., 97209-3922
503-228-5657
info@streetroots.org
www.streetroots.org

WRITE AROUND PORTLAND

Write Around Portland (WRAP) helps low-income and isolated individuals use writing to improve their lives. In the fall and spring, the nonprofit WRAP holds ten-week writing workshops. In the summer, WRAP brings five-week workshops to a low-income neighborhood, publishes anthologies of the work (available online and in local bookstores), and publishes a twice-yearly tabloid, *Free Write*. Publications, readings, and workshops offer a respectful and safe environment in which to write and share. How to get involved: trained volunteers facilitate workshops. Other volunteers assist with graphic design, record-keeping, public relations, childcare, transportation, and management of community events. Accepts donations of journals, pens, gift certificates for food at workshops, TriMet passes, and printing and binding of participant manuscripts.

917 SW Oak St., Suite 406, 97205
503-796-9224
info@writearound.org
www.writearound.org

► Publications

Stay abreast of the latest book-related news and events in Portland by reading these publications:

@YOURLIBRARY

Multnomah County Library publishes an eight-page, tabloid-style newsletter called *@yourlibrary* three times a year and mails it to every county household with a library cardholder. Includes a sampling of hundreds of free library programs for children, teens, adults, and families. Highlights annual events, such as Everybody Reads, the Children's Author Lecture, and the African-American Read-In. Read *@yourlibrary* online at the Web address below or pick up a copy at any branch. Each branch also publishes its own one-page events calendar. Check out the library's searchable "Event Finder" online at www.multcolib .org/events/.

205 NE Russell St., 97212-3796
503-988-6129
careyb@multcolib.org
www.multcolib.org/about/i-pubs.html

GRANDMA'S BOOK LETTER

In this free, independent quarterly newsletter, Kaye J. Exo recommends outstanding books for children, teens, and young adults. The four-page *Grandma's Book Letter* focuses on titles that explore multicultural themes, the environment, and peacemaking. In 2005, *Grandma's Book Letter* added a companion Web site, from which back issues can be downloaded.

P.O. Box 3797, 97208-3797
503-284-3971
kxo@hevanet.com
www.grandmasbookletter.com

INK

Ink, Powell's Books literary journal and calendar of author readings and events, is one the best literary periodicals on the planet, and it's *free*. Published since May 2004, this colorful monthly features exclusive essays by authors; a foldout calendar of readings, workshops, and book groups at all Powell's locations; exclusive author interviews (the likes of John Irving, Richard Ford, Jane Smiley, and Zadie Smith); and author Q&As. It belongs on the refrigerator door of every reader's home. *Ink* doubles nicely as giftwrap for book giving. *Ink* is available at all Powell's locations. Archive of author interviews and Q&A also available online.

1005 W Burnside St., 97209
503-228-4651
www.powells.com/ink

THE OREGONIAN

Most complete coverage of the Portland literary scene and the best reviews of regional literature are led by Books Editor Jeff Baker. See the Sunday edition, inside the *O!* section. Features include local and national bestsellers, library news, local poetry, editors' picks, and a day-by-day literary calendar for the week ahead.

1320 SW Broadway, 97201
503-221-8165
www.oregonlive.com/books

THE PORTLAND MERCURY

Free every Thursday. See starred notices in the *Theater*, *Books*, *Visual Arts* pages for recommended readings. Also publishes book reviews.

605 NE 21st Ave., Suite 200, 97232
503-294-0840
events@portlandmercury.com
www.portlandmercury.com

PORTLAND TRIBUNE

Free every Tuesday and Friday. Freelancers critique books on Fridays in the *Weekend!Events* section. Highlights Portland reading events.

6605 SE Lake Road, Portland 97222
503-226-6397
503-226-7042
www.portlandtribune.com

WILLAMETTE WEEK

Since Portland is the City of Readers, it only makes sense that our very own *free* alternative weekly newspaper would be a Pulitzer Prize winner. Book lovers will appreciate "New Books Plucked from the Publishing Fringes" as well as the "Books" listings of author readings and literary events around the metropolis. Reading for a rainy day: dig through its online archive and check out "Portland, They Wrote: Ten Authors, Ten Stories, One City," an outstanding cover story from September 1, 2004, that included essays by Diana Abu-Jaber, Walt Curtis, Brian Doyle, April Henry, and Christopher Zinn. Another roundup on March 6, 2003, included Anthony Swofford, Larry Colton, Kevin Sampsell, Tom Spanbauer, Sandra Stone, Phillip Margolin, Rochelle Hart, and Zoe Trope.

2220 NW Quimby St., 97210
503-243-2122 or 503-243-4366
www.wweek.com

► Radio

KBOO

Barbara LaMorticella and Portland poet Walt Curtis co-host "The Talking Earth," a poetry program that airs Mondays, 10 p.m.–11 p.m., on nonprofit radio station KBOO (90.7 FM, Portland).

20 SE 8th Ave., 97214
503-231-8032
www.kboo.fm

► Reading Communities/Book Groups

FRIENDS OF MYSTERY

The Friends of Mystery reading group meets at 7 p.m. on the third Wednesday of each month at Murder by the Book, 3210 SE

Hawthorne Blvd. Volunteer moderator leads discussion. Dinner preceding is at 5:45 p.m. at Fu-Jin, 3549 SE Hawthorne Blvd.

P.O. Box 8251, 97207
503-241-0759
info@friendsofmystery.org
www.friendsofmystery.org

ONLINE BOOK CLUBS

Free. Delivers a five-minute portion of a book by e-mail each day. You'll read two to three chapters each week. Available titles: pre-publication, nonfiction, fiction, business, teen, mystery, romance, horror, and science fiction.

Multnomah County Library
www.dearreader.com/library/multnomah

PAGETURNERS

Pageturners, Multnomah County Library's book discussion group, meets monthly at most libraries. (Can't make it to the library? See information above about OnLine Book Clubs.) Groups for adults, kids, and families. Jackie Moyer Fischer, author of *An Egg on Three Sticks*, visited in summer 2005. See the Web site for current calendar and title list.

Multnomah County Library
www.multcolib.org/books/groups

STORYTIMES

At every neighborhood library, Multnomah County Library offers stories, songs, games, and seasonal crafts for babies, toddlers, and preschoolers and their parents.

Multnomah County Library
www.multcolib.org/events/storytime.html

TALK IT UP!

Provides online resources for starting and running a book group for children. More than 150 discussion guides to use with specific books. Created in part with funds from the Oregon State Library.

Multnomah County Library
www.multcolib.org/talk

► Volunteer Opportunities

BOOKS TO OREGON PRISONERS, PORTLAND BOOKS TO PRISONERS

Portland Books to Prisoners and Books to Oregon Prisoners are sister organizations. Both need volunteers and book donations. Some volunteering opportunities include answering book-request letters from Oregon prisoners in state or federal prisons and assembling packages for them. Donations and volunteers are welcome anytime. For a $5 donation, anyone can select two books from the Reflections Mirror-Image Bookstore catalog for delivery to a prisoner. Book donations can be made at the following locations:

- Laughing Horse Books, 12 NE 10th Ave.
- In Other Words, 8 NE Killingsworth St.
- Vinnie's Pizza, 236 N Killingsworth St.
- Rocco's Pizza and Pasta, 949 SW Oak St.

Reflections Mirror-Image Bookstore,
330 N Killingsworth St., 97217
503-288-9003
pdxbookstoprisoners@riseup.net
www.bookstoprisoners.org

MULTNOMAH COUNTY LIBRARY

It's easy to find out about being a volunteer for your local Portland library branch. Multnomah County Library's site explains how you can join the one thousand–plus children and adults each year who support our libraries by volunteering. Rewarding opportunities for English and Spanish speakers usually include working with children and teens, assisting users with new technology, reading to seniors at care facilities, and helping customers at Multnomah County Library's Title Wave Used Bookstore at 216 NE Knott St.

503-988-5731
libvols@multcolib.org
www.multcolib.org/vol

START MAKING A READER TODAY

Each SMART adult volunteer reads with two public elementary schoolchildren for one hour per week throughout the school year. The children, who range from kindergarten to third grade, receive two books each month to keep and read with their families. Since 1992, SMART has provided 2.1 million volunteer hours to 90,000 Oregon children and donated 1.3 million books. Apply online to volunteer.

219 NW 12th Ave., Suite 203, 97209
1-877-598-4633
smart@getsmartoregon.org
www.getsmartoregon.org

VOLUNTEER LITERACY TUTOR PROGRAM

For adults who read below an eighth-grade level, or refugees and immigrants whose first language is not English, the Volunteer Literacy Tutor Program at Portland Community College is a considerable resource. The program matches more than eight hundred volunteers with individual students or small groups at sites citywide, and the attention results in basic skill achievement, translating to employability, college readiness, or better quality of life in general. Volunteering is serious business—you'll need to complete seventeen hours of training—but the payoff is well worth it. You can also donate; proceeds go to maintain a lending library of texts and resources at each site.

Portland Community College, sites citywide
503-244-6111, ext. 3700
literacy@pcc.edu
www.pcc.edu/resources/tutoring/volunteer

PART FOUR

Buy Locally: Portland Bookstores

A GOLDEN AGE OF READING has arrived in Portland, where book lovers have more than a hundred shops from which to choose. Per capita, this city of a half-million residents boasts more bookstores than Chicago, New York, Philadelphia, or Washington, D.C. And it's easy to visit several shops in a single day. Portland is one of the most bike-friendly cities in the United States, and public transportation—even on weekends—is convenient, not to mention *free* in the downtown core.

Portland bookstores range in size, scope, ambition, and personality from Powell's City of Books—a former Nash Automobile dealership where more than one million new and used volumes are parked side-by-side in 3,500 sections—to neighborhood shops such as Wallace Books, a cozy 1925 bungalow in Southeast Portland that bursts with 100,000 titles and extraordinary service.

For local residents, going on a pub-style crawl of bookstores in unfamiliar neighborhoods is a brilliant way to energize your literary life and grow your appreciation of Portland's diversity. East-siders who haven't visited Annie Bloom's Books will discover the enchantment of Multnomah Village in Southwest Portland. West-siders can experience the feel of a small town with a trip north to St. Johns Booksellers.

Another way to deepen your appreciation of Portland is to tour its specialty bookstores. Begin with a trip to the Humboldt neighborhood in Northeast Portland, where Talking Drum Book Store sets the stage for the local African-American literary scene. Nearby is In Other Words, one of the few nonprofit feminist bookstores in the United States. Then travel south toward Burnside Street, where you'll find Laughing Horse Books, an all-volunteer bookstore devoted to social change. And plan an outing to the labyrinthine New Renaissance Bookshop in Northwest Portland, a magical assembly of three classic Portland houses where thousands of spiritual and personal-growth titles await.

Warning for book hounds who put themselves on auto-pilot for Powell's when they head downtown: You'll kick yourself repeatedly for not having explored the eerie hollows of Great Northwest Bookstore, an 1890 church on Southwest First Avenue, where a huge congregation of Western literature and Americana assembles. A second wave of flogging will ensue after you've enjoyed the intimate scale, plus the companionship of a labrador named Charlie, at the Looking Glass Bookstore at 3rd and Taylor. And when you rediscover the dusty charm of leafing through the past at Cameron's Books and Magazines at 3rd and Stark, you'll be ready to assign yourself to detention. (However, if you're an adult, I'd recommend confining yourself with a book at the Detention Bar inside McMenamins Kennedy School.)

Regardless of where you search for your books, remember that Portland's literary landscape is varied and has something for everyone. We readers have our own book-browsing preferences. Some prefer bustling and stimulating, while others prefer quiet and contemplative. Tell us about your favorite local spot to buy books at the *City of Readers* Web site, www.cityofreaders.com.

► New

AGAPÉ

Opened in 1978, this Buckman neighborhood independent has carved out a niche in Pentecostal and charismatic titles. Owner Larry Holloway, a Portland resident since 1961 and onetime executive of the erstwhile Lipman and Wolf Department Store, sells new Christian titles, and he stocks a small used-book room. Sections are organized by authors, including Charles Capps, Yongi Cho, Ken Copeland, Ken Hagin, T. D. Jakes, and Joyce Meyer. Other sections include Bible studies, biography, children, evangelism, and fiction. Agapé is the only Christian bookstore that rents videos and DVDs. Holloway guarantees next-day delivery of special orders.

1711 SE Hawthorne Blvd.
503-236-3949

agapebooks@hevanet.com
Monday–Saturday, 10 a.m.–6 p.m.
Bus: 14-Hawthorne

ANNIE BLOOM'S BOOKS

The handmade sign at the back of the store above the children's section captures the personality of this Multnomah Village shop: "Think Local First." Annie Bloom's packs a whollop of personality, selection, and services that draws a lively flow of loyal customers. Affable, knowledgeable, attentive booksellers make visiting this bookstore a pleasure. The smartly organized store stacks folding metal chairs for readings under the bargain books

IN FULL BLOOM—Multnomah Village in Southwest Portland enjoys a vibrant literary scene at Annie Bloom's Books.

table. Linger in a comfortable reading chair next to the picture window. See the staff-favorites table for fiction, history, mystery, and cooking recommendations. See the store's Web site for author appearances and store events. Annie Bloom's newsletter publishes book reviews by the staff. Annie Bloom's only shortcoming is that Oscar, the black bookstore cat, who mingles among customers like a warm host, is unable to serve the complimentary coffee and tea himself. Free gift wrapping.

7834 SW Capitol Highway
503-246-0053
books@anniesblooms.com
www.annieblooms.com
Daily, 9 a.m.–10 p.m.
Bus: 44-Capitol Highway, 45-Garden Home

BARNES AND NOBLE BOOKSELLERS

A broad selection of Portland- and Oregon-related nonfiction titles is available at both locations. Quick fulfillment of special orders and good follow-up.

Jantzen Beach
1720 Jantzen Beach Center
503-283-2800
www.barnesandnoble.com
Daily, 9 a.m.–10 p.m.
Bus: 6-Martin Luther King Jr. Blvd.

Lloyd Center

1317 Lloyd Center (at Northeast Halsey Street and 12th Avenue)
503-249-0800
www.barnesandnoble.com
Monday–Saturday, 9 a.m.–10 p.m.; Sunday, 10 a.m.–7 p.m.
Bus: 8-Northeast 15th Avenue, 10-Northeast 33rd Avenue,
70-Northeast 12th Avenue, MAX Light Rail

BORDERS

Downtown cube dwellers escape here at lunch to reclaim their souls. Attentive staff delivers consistently superior customer service and bookish banter. Quiet, relaxing coffee shop looks out on the hustle and bustle of Yamhill. The 3rd Avenue store extends a 20 percent discount to local businesses. Big selection of local and literary periodicals, too.

Downtown

708 SW 3rd Ave.
503-220-5911
Monday–Saturday, 9 a.m.–9 p.m.; Sunday, 10 a.m.–7 p.m.
Bus: MAX Light Rail, any bus to downtown

Borders Express

Pioneer Place, 700 SW 5th Ave.
503-274-2728
www.bordersstores.com
Monday–Friday, 9:30 a.m.–9 p.m.; Saturday, 9:30 a.m.–7 p.m.;
Sunday, 11 a.m.–6 p.m.
Bus: MAX Light Rail, any bus to downtown

BRIDGE CITY COMICS

This funky shop fits right in on creative Mississippi Avenue. Bright yellow-and-orange walls and garage door–size windows break the stereotype of comic book haunts. Knowledgeable and cheery owner Michael Ring, who learned to read with help from *Spiderman*, has fulfilled a lifelong dream of selling comics. Sections include select publishers—Dark Horse, Marvel, DC Vertigo—as well as independents, such as locals Top Shelf Productions and Oni Press. There are stacks for "Young Readers" and "Staff Picks." Find Ring's favorites, including obscure series, under the "Comics for the People" sign.

The highlight of the store is its Portland section, featuring artists and writers from the City of Roses. Check out *Local*, about a young woman's misadventures in various U.S. cities— the first issue set in Portland with nice renderings of Union Station and Northwest Portland landmarks. There's also *Pigtale*, which places its boy–hero, would-be detective on familiar Portland streets. Ring echoes what other comics insiders in town say: Portland is second only to New York for comics professionals. Bridge City also stocks graphic novels and trade paperback collections. Used-book trade-in program and subscription services available. Original comic art on display is worth a visit.

3725 N Mississippi Ave.
503-282-5484
info@bridgecitycomics.com
www.bridgecitycomics.com

Tuesday–Saturday, 11 a.m.–7 p.m.; Sunday, noon–5 p.m.; Monday, closed
Bus: 4-Fessenden, MAX Light Rail Yellow Line (Albina/
Mississippi stop)

BRIDGETOWN HOBBIES AND GAMES

Planes, trains, and automobiles! You'll find a sophisticated and extensive selection of books for modelers, gamers, and history buffs. Easy-to-browse listings by hobby category available online.

3350 NE Sandy Blvd.
503-234-1881
www.bthobbies.com
Daily, 10 a.m.–6 p.m.
Bus: 12-Sandy Boulevard

BROADWAY BOOKS

Founded in 1992 by longtime Northeast Portland resident Roberta Dyer, who has thirty-five years of experience in the book business. Fifteen thousand titles. Strengths: new fiction, biography. Most popular: trade paperback fiction. Stop by for Tuesday evening readings. Don't be shy about special orders and gift wrapping—they're free. "We are rabid supporters of our local schools," said Dyer. "We are local, local, local!" Broadway Books is a member of Northeast Broadway Business Association and American Booksellers for Freedom of Expression. Obvious oversight: At the release party for *Harry Potter and the Half-Blood Prince*, the Broadway Books sorting hat placed my wife in Slytherin.

1714 NE Broadway
503-282-1726
bookbroads@aol.com
Monday–Saturday, 10 a.m.–9 p.m., Sunday, noon–5 p.m.
Bus: 9-Broadway

ON BROADWAY—Affable service, late hours, and excellent recommendations beckon Portland readers to Broadway Books in Northeast Portland.

A CHILDREN'S PLACE

For more than thirty years, owner Pamela Erlandson has been helping Portland parents and their children connect with books. Offers a broad selection of titles: newborns through young adults, parenting and teacher resources, children's music, and games. The shop has special sections for books of the same theme, such as fairy books, books about trains, or Cinderella stories. Offers a 20 percent discount to teachers, librarians, and media specialists for books used at school.

4807 NE Fremont St.
503-284-8294
pam@kidslit.net
Monday–Saturday, 10 a.m.–6 p.m.; Sunday, noon–5 p.m.
Bus: 33-Fremont

CHRISTIAN SUPPLY

Portland businessman Bob Pamplin, Jr., owns a chain of Christian Supply stores in Oregon, Washington, and Idaho, including this Southeast Portland location. Stocks large selection of fiction and nonfiction titles, including Bibles and children's books. Store hosts author appearances—see Web site for schedule.

10209 SE Division St.
503-256-4520
www.christiansupply.net
Monday–Saturday, 10 a.m.–9 p.m.; Sunday, 11 a.m.–6 p.m.
Bus: 4-Division

CIRCUIT RIDER BOOKS

5441 SE Belmont St.
503-234-9625
circuitrider@circuitriderbooks.org
www.circuitriderbooks.org
Call for hours
Bus: 15-Belmont
See "Nonprofit."

COUNTER MEDIA

On the Acorn Block just southeast of Powell's is this shop that sells underground cartoons, graphic novels, erotic photography, vintage magazines, and erotic fiction and nonfiction. Buys vintage erotica (pre-1980) and photos from the 1920s and 1930s.

927 SW Oak St.
503-226-8141
Monday–Saturday, 11 a.m.–7 p.m.; Sunday, noon–6 p.m.
Bus: 20-Burnside/Stark

GIFTS OF THE SPIRIT

Founded by Portland natives Gladys Dieringer, a former Grotto gift store manager who passed away in 2005, and her sister Mary Dieringer. One of three Catholic bookstores in Portland. Stock includes religious books, crucifixes, holy cards, and Christopher medals. The store is happy to fill special orders.

7001 SE 52nd Ave.
503-771-6442
Call for hours
Bus: 71-60th Avenue/122nd Avenue

IN OTHER WORDS, WOMEN'S BOOKS AND RESOURCES

8 NE Killingsworth St.
503-232-6003
othrwrds@teleport.com
www.inotherwords.org
Monday–Friday, 10 a.m.–9 p.m.; Saturday, 10 a.m.–6 p.m.;
Sunday, noon–5 p.m.
Bus: 72-Killingsworth/82nd Avenue
See "Nonprofit."

LAUGHING HORSE BOOKS

12 NE 10th Ave.
503-236-2893
Monday–Saturday, 11 a.m.–7 p.m.; Sunday, call for hours.
Bus: 12-Sandy Blvd., 19-Glisan, 20-Burnside/Stark
See "Nonprofit."

LOOKING GLASS BOOKSTORE

If you'd like a personal literary consultation—sort of like therapy, only much less expensive and much more fun—come to Looking

Glass and meet owner Karin Anna. Caution: This knowledge-able and gracious bookseller likely will introduce you to an international author or poet who might upset your reading routine. Entire staff of this downtown shop is smart and attentive. Looking Glass stocks a broad range of new books, with emphasis on international literature, politics, children's books, environmental issues, alternative health, and spirituality. The shop publishes a monthly newsletter, *Through the Looking Glass*, available in hard copy or by e-mail. Frequent author readings and events. Not incidentally, Anna is a leader in the Campaign for Reader Privacy, a nationwide effort to obtain one million signatures in support of legislation to amend Section 215 of the USA Patriot Act. While you're there, be sure to meet Charlie, the Labrador-in-residence.

---

318 SW Taylor St.
503-227-4760
lookingglassbook@qwest.net
www.lookingglassbookstore.com
Monday–Friday, 9 a.m.–6 p.m.; Saturday, 10 a.m.–6 p.m.;
Sunday, closed
Bus: MAX, any bus to downtown

MOYER'S BOOKSTORE

Conveniently located on the MAX Blue Line and close to Cascade College, Moyer's stocks a select number of Christian titles, with an emphasis on educational resources. What you can't find in the store you're sure to find on its comprehensive Web site.

9842 E Burnside St.
503-774-4633
info@moyersbookstore.com
www.moyersbookstore.com
Monday–Friday, 10 a.m.–5 p.m.; Saturday, 10 a.m.–2 p.m.
Bus: 14–Hawthorne, 17–Holgate

MURDER BY THE BOOK

The scene for crime readers is here on Portland's Boulevard of Books. Owners Jill Hinckley (who founded the business in

CRIME SCENE—The headquarters for local mystery readers is Murder by the Book, where armchair detectives can uncover clues to excellent whodunits.

1983) and Carolyn Lane (who joined in 1984) have adroitly organized ten thousand new and used mysteries in nearly thirty sections, from "On the Home Front" (Pacific Northwest authors or locations) and "Cherchez La Femme" (by and about modern women) to "Off the Wall" (humor) and "Shot On Location" (foreign settings). Innovative services—such as Murder Book by Book, which alerts patrons when they attempt to buy the same book twice—have built a loyal customer base. Come in with just a partial clue to what you're looking for and the staff's one hundred years of combined experience will turn up the right suspect more quickly than Interpol. Frequent author appearances updated at the shop's Web site. One of the best books in the shop doesn't have a plot yet does offer a riveting forty-four-page list of recommended reads, including selected award winners: Murder by the Book's own *Two Decades of Great Mysteries*, $4.95. Also publishes *Murder by the Bye* newsletter monthly.

3210 SE Hawthorne Blvd.
503-232-9995
books@mbtb.com
www.mbtb.com
Monday–Saturday, 10 a.m.–6:30 p.m.; Sunday, 11 a.m.–5 p.m.
Bus: 14–Hawthorne

NEW RENAISSANCE BOOKSHOP

No matter which path you're on, your imagination—and all your senses—will be captured by this delightful maze of three Victorian beauties in Northwest Portland. Browse through sixteen thousand new books in a broad range of spiritual and personal-growth subjects, from Native American spirituality and Kabbalah to hypnosis and handwriting analysis. Upstairs holds three thousand used books, a meditation chapel, and home furnishings. You'll find soothing music and attentive staff. An adjacent fourth building sets the stage for an ambitious offering of author appearances, lectures, and workshops.

1338 NW 23rd Ave.
503-224-4929
orders@newrenbooks.com
www.newrenbooks.com
Monday–Thursday, 10 a.m.–9 p.m.; Friday, 10 a.m.–9:30 p.m.;
Saturday, 10 a.m.–9 p.m.; Sunday, 10 a.m.–6 p.m.
Bus: 15-Northwest 23rd Avenue, 77-Broadway/Halsey,
Portland Streetcar

PILGRIM DISCOUNT

The ultimate Christian supply store, Pilgrim Discount stocks an impressive selection of new and used titles, plus an entire room devoted to "outlet bargains." You'll also find videos, Bible accessories, inspirational gifts, and new and used music. Used book and music buyer in store—call first.

9003 SE Stark St.
503-255-7283, 1-800-678-5377
service@pilgrimdiscount.com
www.pilgrimdiscount.com

Tuesday–Thursday, 10 a.m.–6 p.m.; Friday, 10 a.m.–7 p.m.; Saturday,
10 a.m.–5 p.m.; Sunday–Monday, closed
Bus: 15-Belmont

POWELL'S BOOKS AT PORTLAND INTERNATIONAL AIRPORT

Same cargo as Powell's mother ship on Burnside, yet on a smaller and sometimes more enjoyable deck: used books mixed with new. Powell's operates three shops at the airport: Oregon Market and C and D concourses. Book buying by drop-off. It usually takes two days for a buyer to assess. Seller returns to pick up books, trade slip, or cash.

7000 NE Airport Way, Suite 2250
503-249-1950
help@powells.com
www.powells.com
Oregon Market: Sunday–Friday, 6 a.m.–10 p.m.; Saturday,
5 a.m.–8 p.m.; Concourse C: Sunday–Wednesday, 6 a.m.–8 p.m.;
Thursday–Saturday, 5 a.m.–8 p.m.; Concourse D: Sunday–Friday,
5 a.m.–4:20 p.m.; Saturday, 5 a.m.–3:30 p.m.
Bus: MAX Light Rail Red Line

POWELL'S BOOKS FOR HOME AND GARDEN

Dig in to this rich offering of indoor and outdoor know-how. Titles include knitting, jewelry making, woodworking, landscape design, and gardening. Blended in are cooking utensils, dishes, linens, and garden tools. Caution: An enticing gourmet food shop called Pastaworks looms next door.

3747 SE Hawthorne Blvd.
503-228-4651
help@powells.com
www.powells.com
Monday–Saturday, 9 a.m.–9 p.m.; Sunday, 9 a.m.–8 p.m.; book buying, daily, 10 a.m.–5:30 p.m.
Bus: 14-Hawthorne, 75-39th Avenue/Lombard

POWELL'S BOOKS ON HAWTHORNE

More than 200,000 new and used volumes shelved in three rooms, each named for local Southeast Portland streets (Hawthorne, Madison) and the nearby extinct volcano (Tabor). Pick up a map that guides you to its bounty of 255 sections, from American Sign Language at Tiger Island in the Hawthorne Room to Leftist Studies in the Madison Room. Chimps Rollerskating, Fancy Dancing, Organ Donating Hobbies, and Pants Management sections are a bit thin.

3723 SE Hawthorne Blvd.
503-238-1668
help@powells.com
www.powells.com
Monday–Thursday, 9 a.m.–10 p.m.; Friday–Saturday, 9 a.m.–11 p.m.; Sunday, 9 a.m.–9 p.m.; book buying, daily, 9 a.m.–10 p.m.
Bus: 14-Hawthorne, 75-39th Avenue/Lombard

If you're a local, close your eyes and try to imagine Portland without Powell's City of Books.... Neither can I. So, at the top of your list of questions about Powell's should not be, "Whose ashes are buried in The Pillar of Books?" but rather, "Will Michael Powell ever sell Powell's?" And the answer, issued directly from the man himself, is "No." In fact, the forward-thinking Grant High School graduate has been working on a succession plan for several years. He will turn the business over to his daughter, Emily Powell, as soon as 2010.

Now, close your eyes and try to imagine a sunny day—in fact, a sunny *Saturday*—in the middle of a dreary Portland winter. Now,

BOOKLAND—One of the Seven Wonders of the Literary World, Powell's Books on Burnside boasts more than one million volumes in thirty-five hundred subject areas.

where would you expect to find the most people in town gathered on this auspicious occasion? Outside? Not in Portland. Here, the biggest crowd in Portland on a sunny Saturday in the middle of a cold and wet winter can be found inside Powell's City of Books.

To visitors: If you're making your first pilgrimage to the City of Books, prepare as you would for a trip to the City of Lights. Like Paris, Powell's is sprawling and chaotic (on weekends and especially during the holidays). Plan your trip (there's a store map online, or a foldout at the information desk when you arrive), wear comfortable shoes, and leave plenty of room in your luggage for souvenirs. Getting there: limited, free off-street parking is available on 10th and in the Powell's garage on 11th. Your best bet is taking the Portland Streetcar to the Couch Street stop. The classic Powell's entrance is 10th and Burnside, where the windows provide a gallery of odd and entertaining titles. Once inside, your best hope is to schedule a time and place to meet your friends and loved ones in the distant future. You have nearly seventy thousand square feet on three floors to explore. More than one million new and used books are shelved side by side in 122 major subject areas and more than 3,500 subsections. (The only titles you won't find here are computer books, which are located two blocks east at Powell's Technical Books.) Don't miss the Small Press section on the north wall of the Blue Room. Check out chalkboards on the east side of the second floor for recent literary deaths and prizes. When you leave—if you leave—head out through the Orange Room and the doors at 11th and Couch and lean on The Pillar of Books. If you haven't read at least one of the eight books whose titles are inscribed there, immediately go back inside.

1005 W Burnside St.
503-228-4651
help@powells.com
www.powells.com
Daily, 9 a.m.–11 p.m.; book buying, daily, 9 a.m.–8:30 p.m.
Bus: 20-Burnside/Stark, Portland Streetcar

POWELL'S TECHNICAL BOOKS

Item no. 1: The cross street, "Couch," rhymes with "pooch" or "hooch." While you browse through the titles on mathematics, computers, physics, electronics, and engineering, make sure you meet Fup, the seventeen-year-old store cat. She has her own business card and e-mail address: fup@powells.com. Used-book sellers: Look for "Used Technical Books We Always Want," with titles such as *Zen of Assembly Language* and *Kent's Mechanical Engineers Handbook*, 12th edition. This Powell's store publishes its own free quarterly newsletter, *Technica*, which features book reviews and photos of author events. *Technica* is also available electronically; just e-mail technica@technical.powells .com. Don't forget to pick up your Fup coloring sheet.

33 NW Park Ave. (at Couch Street)
503-228-4651, 1-800-878-7323
help@powells.com
www.powells.com
Monday–Saturday, 9 a.m.–9 p.m.; Sunday, 11 a.m.–7 p.m.; book buying, daily, 11 a.m.–7 p.m.
Bus: 20-Burnside/Stark, Portland Streetcar

READING FRENZY

A stone's throw from the largest independent bookstore on Earth is one of its smallest. More than proximity ties them. Each store has auto-industry ancestors. Powell's City of Books occupies a former dealership, while decade-old Reading Frenzy began in the office of a body shop. Lesson: If you want to open a successful bookstore here, watch for a parts store or gas station to lease its space. Owner Chloe Eudaly, co-founder of Portland's Independent Publishing Resource Center, offers locally self-published magazines and chapbooks. Eudaly's Show and Tell Press, founded in 2006, publishes *Crap Hound*, a clip art zine. Among the popular titles is Chris Ware's *Jimmy Carrigan: The Smartest Kid on Earth*.

921 SW Oak St.
503-274-1449
general@readingfrenzy.com
www.readingfrenzy.com
Monday–Saturday, 11 a.m.–7 p.m.; Sunday, noon–6 p.m.
Bus: 20-Burnside/Stark, Portland Streetcar

REFLECTIONS MIRROR-IMAGE BOOKSTORE

Owner O. B. Hill moved his small African-American bookstore, which formerly shared space with nearby Reflections Coffee House, to this corner shop near Jefferson High School in December 2004. He stocks primarily new titles by black writers, including local authors such as Rochell D. Hart and others from the Pacific Northwest. Strong poetry selection. Also offered are

OUTREACH—O. B. Hill, owner of Reflections Mirror-Image Bookstore on North Killingsworth Street, volunteers for Books to Oregon Prisoners.

used books and rentals. Hill collaborates with the Books to Oregon Prisoners project (see "Volunteer Opportunities" in "Act Locally") and accepts donations of new and used books for the nonprofit program.

330 N Killingsworth St. (at Vancouver Avenue)
503-288-9003
Monday–Thursday, 10 a.m.–1 p.m., 3 p.m.–6 p.m.; closed Friday;
Saturday, 10 a.m.–6 p.m.; closed Sunday
Bus: 72-Killingsworth/82nd Avenue

SERENITY SHOP

Originally located in a chicken barn in Gresham, Serenity Shop moved to this 1909 Richmond neighborhood house in 1980.

Counselor Judy Wallace, who has owned the shop for seventeen years, stocks one thousand books on addictions, emotional issues, and spiritual growth as well as a selection of encouraging cards and gifts. Popular items include 12-step medallions, jewelry, and bumper stickers. Self-help referrals and resources also are available. "It's a wonderful place to come and get some serenity," says Wallace.

3212 SE Division St.
503-235-3383
serenity@serenityshop.com
www.serenityshop.com
Monday–Friday, 10 a.m.–6 p.m.; Sunday, noon–5 p.m.
Bus: 4-Division

STEINER STOREHOUSE

All anthroposophical titles—you know, books about the philosophy or spiritual science movement founded by Rudolf Steiner. Steiner Storehouse is owned by Dr. John Takacs, who operates an adjacent osteopathic medical clinic. Stocks six hundred titles on education and parenting, children's literature, estoric studies, medicine and health, gardening, and art.

5915 SE Division St., Suite 2
503-777-1251
info@steinerstorehouse.com
www.steinerstorehouse.com

Monday–Saturday, 9 a.m.–5 p.m.
Bus: 4–Division

ST. JOHNS BOOKSELLERS

Néna Rawdah and Liz Dorman accomplished what many Powell's employees dream of doing. They opened their own bookstore, with the help of a Mercy Corps small-business loan, on June 25, 2005. Rawdah, originally from Dallas, Texas, and Dorman, who hails from Memphis, Tennessee, met in 1996 at Powell's City of Books, where Rawdah served as a science fiction section specialist and Dorman worked in the phone orders department. Preparing to take over the 1925 shop formerly occupied by Paperbacks Etc., the duo solicited input from St. Johns residents, who said they wanted children's books. The result: 20 percent of their 2,300 square feet is devoted to titles for tots, and the first book they sold was *Pat the Bunny* by Dorothy Kunhardt. They began with 1,700 books and will expand to five thousand. Like their alma mater, they shelve new and used side by side. Don't miss nearby: beautiful, refurbished manual typewriters at Blue Moon Camera and Machine (www.bluemooncamera.com), 8417 N Lombard St.

8622 N Lombard St.
503-283-0032
info@stjohnsbooks.com, orders@stjohnsbooks.com
www.stjohnsbooks.com
Tuesday–Sunday, 10 a.m.–6 p.m.

Bus: 4-Fessenden, 17-Northwest 21st Avenue/St. Helens Road,
40-Mocks Crest, 75-39th Avenue/Lombard

TALKING DRUM BOOKSTORE AND
REFLECTIONS COFFEE HOUSE

In the heart of Portland's African-American cultural community, Talking Drum Book Store stocks Afrocentric fiction and nonfiction, cards, and gifts. You're welcome to sip coffee from Reflections Coffee House while you browse. Owner Gloria McMurtry hosts open-mike poetry (Wednesdays), author appearances, a book club, and art exhibitions. Staged Readings Theatre presents shows at 8 p.m. on the first Friday and Saturday of each month; tickets are $8 at the door. Plenty of free, off-street parking under cover at the Walnut Park Retail Center.

446 NE Killingsworth St. (at Martin Luther King Jr. Boulevard)
503-288-4106
talkingdrumbooks@att.net
Monday–Saturday, 7 a.m.–6 p.m.; closed Sunday
Bus: 6-Martin Luther King Jr. Blvd., 72-Killingsworth/
82nd Avenue

TRANG'S BOOKS

Catering to Portland's Vietnamese cultural community, Trang's Books stocks books, magazines, videos, and music. Valuable resources for anyone planning a trip to Vietnam or just looking to enrich his or her understanding of Vietnamese culture. Some of the pop-culture magazines are written in English. Also carries Vietnamese–English translation volumes. Pick up a book and enjoy some Pho in the restaurant just below the store.

8211 NE Brazee, Suite H (on 82nd Avenue, near
Interstate 84)
503-255-6626
Daily, 11 a.m.–8 p.m.
Bus: 72-Killingsworth /82nd Avenue

TWENTY-THIRD AVENUE BOOKS

If you're a visitor to Portland and you only have time to visit two or three of the city's bookshops, put Twenty-Third Avenue Books at the top of your list. Just hop on the streetcar to Nob Hill and deboard at Lovejoy Street. Long before "Trendy Third" hit the map, this bookshop became a hotspot for discriminating readers and a destination for touring writers. Established in 1980, this first-rate store is a defining feature of Nob Hill's personality. Twenty-Third Avenue Books stocks a careful selection of contemporary fiction, mysteries, and classics. The store is noted for its gay and lesbian fiction section. While you're there, read the Coffee House Press poster of Jane Smiley's "The Worth of a Bookstore." Search the walls for a picture of your favorite author among the more than 130 autographed photos: from the devil-horned Chuck Palahniuk to Eugene's Lauren Kessler, Seattle's Earl Emerson, and Portland's Tom Spanbauer. Classical music and attentive booksellers are icing on the cake. Before you leave: Pose with the picture of Bernard, the rascally bookshop owner from the British sitcom "Black Books." Hint to shop's quality: Author David Sedaris visits when he's in town.

1015 NW 23rd Ave.
503-224-5097
bookson23rd@aol.com
www.23rdavebooks.com
Monday–Thursday, 9:30 a.m.–7 p.m.; Friday, 9:30 a.m.–8 p.m.,
Saturday, 10 a.m.–8 p.m.; Sunday, 10:30 a.m.–7 p.m.
Bus: 15–NW 23rd Avenue, 77–Broadway/Halsey,
Portland Streetcar

WALLACE BOOKS

This bungalow bookshop, a favorite of Tom McCall biographer and Pulitzer Prize–winning journalist Brent Walth, is the perfect reason to venture out of your book-hunting routine to visit the Sellwood Moreland neighborhood. Just south of Bybee Boulevard, Wallace Books is perhaps best defined by what it doesn't have: a recorded message on its phone, a Web site, magazines, books on tape, videos and DVDs, T-shirts, water bottles, literary knicknacks, or a coffee shop. Inside this cozy cottage are new and used books shelved together from floor to ceiling, two deep in the front-room fiction section. Wallace Books stocks an excellent selection of contemporary and classic fiction and maintains one of the broadest Pacific Northwest authors sections among all Portland bookshops. Julie Wallace, who earned her bookselling stripes at Powell's Books in Beaverton, opened the shop in 1997. Unlike some bookstores where the staff doesn't speak until spoken to, booksellers here approach customers and offer service. They provide quick, knowledgeable price quotes on out-of-print titles. Bring your own coffee and camp out. This bookstore brews its own magical atmosphere.

7241 SE Milwaukie Ave.
503-235-7350
jwallace@wallacebooks.net
Daily, 10 a.m.–7 p.m.
Bus: 19-Woodstock, 70-12th Avenue

► Used and Rare

AGAPÉ

See "New."

ARMCHAIR BOOKSTORE

Straight out of the movie *Pulp Fiction* and just north of Brooklyn Park, this is one of Portland's smallest used paperback and magazine shops. The aisles are cramped, so, as a sign inside suggests, "If you have nothing to do, do not do it here." Cash only.

3205 SE Milwaukie Ave.
503-238-6680
Monday–Friday, 10 a.m.–7 p.m.; Saturday, 10 a.m.–6 p.m.;
Sunday, closed
Bus: 19-Woodstock

CAMERON'S BOOKS AND MAGAZINES

Nowhere else can you step into the display window of an 1890 building and see things from a mannequin's perspective, as well as browse through children's, sports, and reference books. Nestled under the venerable Golden Dragon Restaurant downtown on 3rd and Stark is Portland's oldest bookstore. Cameron's will celebrate its seventieth birthday in 2008. The store carries about 100,000 books, current magazines, and vintage magazines, some stored at a warehouse. Web site lists new acquisitions ("Just In") and purchase needs ("In Search Of"). Check racks of inexpensive paperbacks outside the entrance.

336 SW 3rd Ave. (at Stark Street)
503-228-2391
info@cameronsbooks.com
www.cameronsbooks.com
Monday–Saturday, 10 a.m.–6 p.m.; Sunday, noon–4 p.m.
Bus: MAX, any bus to downtown

DAEDALUS BOOKS

Daedalus Books is, hands down, Portland's most beautifully designed bookshop, if not the city's most aesthetically pleasing retail interior, period. Add the tantalizing aroma from Ken's Artisan Bakery next door, and Daedalus casts a spell on its visitors. Big selection of scholarly titles in classical studies, history, linguistics, literary studies, Judaica, medicine, and philosophy. Check out the Bibliography, Film, and History of

Books sections. If the title you're pining for isn't on the shelf, ask the friendly, online-savvy staff: there's a warehouse attached. Buys used and scholarly books as well as military and music titles.

2074 NW Flanders St.
503-274-7742
daedalus@aracnet.com
www.abebooks.com/home/daedalus
Monday–Friday, 9:30 a.m.–9 p.m.; Saturday, 10 a.m.–9 p.m.;
Sunday, 10:30 a.m.–7 p.m.
Bus: 15-NW 23rd Avenue, 17-NW 21st Avenue/St. Helens Road,
20-Burnside/Stark, Portland Streetcar

DRAGON'S HEAD BOOKS AND GIFTS

This tiny shop in Northeast Portland's Center neighborhood stocks popular fiction and nonfiction, both hardbacks and paperbacks. Seniors save 10 percent on Wednesday.

6016 NE Glisan St.
503-235-5995
www.biblio.com/bookstores/rlholder.html
Tuesday–Wednesday, 9 a.m.–1 p.m.; Thursday–Saturday, noon–7 p.m.;
Sunday, 1 p.m.–7 p.m.
Bus: 19-Glisan, 71-60th Avenue/122nd Avenue, MAX Light Rail
Blue and Red lines

EXCALIBUR BOOKS AND COMICS

Graphic novels, comics, and the best storehouse of knowledge about them in Portland. Owner Peter Fagnant and his daughter, Debbie Fagnant, are enthusiastic and knowledgeable about the city's growing talent pool of comics writers, artists, and publishers. Buys, sells, trades.

2444 SE Hawthorne Blvd.
503-231-7351
info@excaliburcomics.net
www.excaliburcomics.net
Monday–Thursday, 11 a.m.–8 p.m.; Friday–Saturday, 10 a.m.–8 p.m.;
Sunday, 11 a.m.–7 p.m.
Bus: 14-Hawthorne

FUTURE DREAMS BOOKS

Don't judge this Kerns neighborhood bookstore by its cover. Inside is a clean, well-lighted place. Owner Donald Riordan stocks new and used science fiction titles plus thousands of old comics.

2205 E Burnside St.
503-231-8311
fdb@hevanet.com
www.futuredreamsbooks.com
Monday–Tuesday, 10 a.m.–7 p.m.; Wednesday–Friday, 10 a.m.–8 p.m.;
Saturday–Sunday, 11 a.m.–8 p.m.
Bus: 19-Glisan, 20-Burnside/Stark

HIGH CALIBER—Peter Fagnant, owner of Excalibur Books and Comics, and his daughter, Debbie Fagnant, give Portlanders the inside scoop on comics and graphic novels.

GREAT NORTHWEST BOOKSTORE

Welcome to the city's most unusual bookstore setting: an 1890 church—appropriate for a shop that specializes in Western literature and Americana. The front door creaks open, and you could be stepping onto the set of a movie. Owner Phil Wikelund, who started in the business in the early 1970s, had always entertained a fantasy about living in a church, and when he sold his downtown location, he found this former Presbyterian church in the Lair Hill neighborhood. Great Northwest issues a quarterly catalog of more than five hundred unusual titles and is always in the market for Western Americana, Civil War, general history, college texts, and role-playing games such as *Dungeons and Dragons*. Search inventory online. Staff offers professional appraisals for tax or insurance purposes. Great Northwest's most valuable asset is its manager, longtime Portland bookman John Henley, novelist (*The Buchmans*) and instructor at Portland State University.

3314 SW 1st Ave.
503-223-9474

THE GOOD BOOK—This 1890 church in the city's Lair Hill neighborhood houses Great Northwest Bookstore and its huge inventory of Western literature and Americana.

gnworders@greatnorthwestbooks.com
www.greatnorthwestbooks.com
Monday–Friday, 9 a.m.–6 p.m.
Bus: 12-Barbur Boulevard, 43-Taylors Ferry Road, 44-Capitol
Highway, 45-Garden Home

HAWTHORNE BOULEVARD BOOKS

The Pearl really isn't in Northwest Portland. Portland's pearl of used bookshops lies across the Willamette River in Southeast Portland's Sunnyside neighborhood: Hawthorne Boulevard Books. Step into this cozy 1910 bungalow of books, and you'll want to cast your lot with twenty-year owners Roger and Ilse Roberts, if for no other reason than their excellent company. You might also be taken with reading at the round table in the fireplace room. Strengths: Western Americana and books on books. Excellent Northwest section on your right as you enter. Patrons include Michael Powell and John Dunning, author of the *Booked to Die* mystery series, who shops here whenever he's in town and once told a Powell's audience that Hawthorne Boulevard Books is the best shop in town. Used books bought all hours.

3129 SE Hawthorne Blvd.
503-236-3211
hbb@teleport.com
Wednesday–Saturday, 11 a.m.–5 p.m., and by appointment
Bus: 14-Hawthorne

KISS BOOKS

Collectors of publishers' preview copies—a.k.a. advance reader's copies—will find a big selection at this small shop in the Sellwood-Moreland neighborhood. Many low-priced firsts for sale, too.

8317 SE 13th Ave.
503-239-3974
Call for hours
Bus: 70-12th Avenue

LONGFELLOW'S BOOKSTORE

Feels like the 1960s or 1970s at this Hosford-Abernathy neighborhood store. Beautiful selection of modern firsts. Other specialties: West, Pacific Northwest, Oregon, literature, juvenile series, sheet music, back issues of fine magazines. Appraisals, house calls.

1401 SE Division St.
503-239-5222
longfellowspdx@comcast.net
abebooks.com
Monday—Saturday, 12:30 p.m.–5:30 p.m.
Bus: 4-Division

MURDER BY THE BOOK

See "New."

NEW RENAISSANCE BOOKSHOP

See "New."

OLD FRIENDS BOOKS

Enjoy the sounds of classical music while you ogle the shelves at this locally owned shop, which opened in 1995. The smell of freshly brewed coffee from True Brew Espresso holds you close, too. This Brooklyn neighborhood shop boasts ten thousand

PERFECT BLEND—Old Friends Books in the Brooklyn neighborhood combines two Portland favorites: used books and locally roasted, organic coffee.

high-quality volumes and specializes in collectibles and antiques pricing and reference guides (including some new stock). Nice selection of hardcover fiction. Buys nonfiction, especially interested in military history, science, gardening, cooking, and older illustrated books.

_____

3370 SE Milwaukie Ave.
503-231-0301
Daily, 10 a.m.–6 p.m.
Bus: 19-Woodstock

PAPER MOON BOOKS

Forty thousand used books are shelved at this Southeast Belmont shop, open since 1974 in the Sunnyside neighborhood. Specialties include antique children's titles, literature, art, music, and cookbooks. Buyer and appraiser available for house calls.

_____

4707 SE Belmont St.
503-239-8848
paprmoon@europa.com
http://home.europa.com/~paprmoon/
Tuesday–Saturday, 11 a.m.–6 p.m.
Bus: 15-Belmont

POWELL'S BOOKS AT PORTLAND INTERNATIONAL AIRPORT

See "New."

Not all bookshops have a brick-and-mortar storefront. And while Internet-only booksellers are not the focus of *City of Readers*, there's one longtime independent dealer who is a fixture of Portland's literary landscape: Charles Seluzicki.

Seluzicki, who has lived in Portland since 1979, began his Fine and Rare Books service in Baltimore. He started his Fine Press Series at that time and began publishing books and broadsides by poets including Ted Hughes, Charles Simic, Tess Gallagher, Czeslaw Milosz, and Mark Strand.

In the spring of 2006, the Collins Gallery at Central Library held an exhibition of his work, called "Charles Seluzicki: 30 Years as a Fine Press Publisher." The exhibition, which was installed by Jim Carmin, who is the John Wilson Special Collections librarian, included a copy of Portlander Katherine Dunn's *Geek Love*, one of thirty-two copies illustrated and bound by Seattle artist Mare Blocker.

Seluzicki, as do other Portlanders who are Internet-only dealers, sells through the International Association of Antiquarian Booksellers' Web site at www.ilab.org and other online marketplaces.

POWELL'S BOOKS FOR HOME AND GARDEN

See "New."

POWELL'S BOOKS ON HAWTHORNE

See "New."

POWELL'S CITY OF BOOKS

See "New."

POWELL'S TECHNICAL BOOKS

See "New."

SECOND GLANCE BOOKS

Owner Rachelle Markley, a former manager at Barnes and Noble Lloyd Center who likes to read Southern Gothic writers such as William Faulkner and Flannery O'Connor, purchased this Hollywood neighborhood shop (formerly called Author's Books and Publishing Service) in March 2005. She stocks twelve thousand titles, largely paperback. Most popular sections include romance, mystery, and classics. Building fiction and children's section. The store will trade only for high-quality hardbacks and paperbacks, excluding popular fiction hardbacks, and also offers a search service for used and out-of-print titles (charges commission on sale).

4500 NE Sandy Blvd.
503-249-0344
sgbooks@qwest.net
www.abebooks.com
Monday–Friday, 10 a.m.–6 p.m.; Saturday, 10 a.m.–7p.m.; Sunday
11 a.m.–5 p.m.
Bus: 12-Sandy Blvd.; MAX Light Rail to Hollywood/Northeast 42nd
Avenue station

ST. JOHNS BOOKSELLERS

See "New."

WALLACE BOOKS

See "New."

► Nonprofit

ALCOHOLICS ANONYMOUS: PORTLAND AREA INTERGROUP, INC.

Relocated to the Hosford-Abernathy neighborhood in July 2004 after fourteen years on Naito Parkway in Northwest Portland. Carries three hundred Alcoholics Anonymous titles and other materials, including books and speakers on compact disc. Order by phone or e-mail. Managed by Gary Biggers for twelve years.

1212 SE Division St.
503-223-8569

webmaster@portland-aa.org
www.pdxaa.com
Monday–Friday, 9 a.m.–5 p.m.; Saturday, 10 a.m.–9 p.m.; Sunday,
10:30 a.m.–7 p.m.
Bus: 4-Division, 70-12th Avenue

AUDUBON SOCIETY OF PORTLAND NATURE STORE

Nestled in the mossy haven of Forest Park is a wonderful spot to shop for bird feeders, birdseed, and books about much more than just birds. Subjects include Audubon, nature, geology, wildlife, local history and guidebooks, and kids' books. Sit in the over-sized chairs in Heron Hall and check out the great selection of reference books. While you're there, don't forget to take a hike through the sanctuary. Trails are free to the public and open daily from dawn until dusk.

5151 NW Cornell Road
503-292-9453
general@audubonportland.org
www.audubonportland.org
Monday–Saturday, 10 a.m.–6 p.m.; Sunday, 10 a.m.–5 p.m.
Bus: 18-Hillside

CIRCUIT RIDER BOOKS

A unique, mobile Christian book ministry that has served mainline Protestant churches in the Pacific Northwest for twenty years. Provides book tables at conferences and fills individual orders. Specializes in titles from publishers such as Abingdon, Augsburg, Chalice, Fortress, Judson, Morehouse, Pilgrim, and Westminster/John Knox. Incorporated as nonprofit in 2001.

5441 SE Belmont St.
503-234-9625
circuitrider@circuitriderbooks.org
www.circuitriderbooks.org
Call for hours
Bus: 15-Belmont

ETHOS

On the eastern edge of the Kerns neighborhood, tucked inside St. Dimitrios Hall on the main floor of Holy Trinity Greek Orthodox Church, is a unique Portland bookshop. Among the two hundred or so titles are English and Greek-language religious guides, cookbooks, children's books, and language instruction. Also available: icons, jewelry, and Byzantine chants and a cappella recordings. Staffing the shop are volunteers, such as eighty-eight-year-old Christina Koutures, who has belonged to the six-hundred-member parish since childhood.

3131 NE Glisan St.
503-234-0468
Sunday–Friday, 11 a.m.–3 p.m.
Bus: 19-Glisan

ETHOS—In Northeast Portland, the city's smallest bookshop, Ethos, is nestled inside Holy Trinity Greek Orthodox Church.

FRIENDS' LIBRARY STORE

Just inside the entrance to Central Library is a shop devoted to literary-themed merchandise and used books. Friends of the Library opened the store in 1997 in conjunction with the renovated Central Library. Proceeds benefit programs throughout the library system. Stocks a small selection of high-quality used books. Managed by Barbara (Babs) Adamski. New merchandise includes jewelry, T-shirts, tote bags, notebooks, calendars, greeting cards (including a series that features readers and writers by Sherwood, Oregon, artist Deborah Dewit Marchant), color postcards of the renovated library, and prints. Purchase a tax-deductible Friends of the Library membership ($30 individual, $45 family, $20 senior) and receive a 10 percent discount plus admission to opening night of the Friend's dynamite annual used book sale (see "Events" in "Act Locally").

801 SW 10th Ave.
503-988-5911
folstore@europa.com
www.friends-library.org/store
Tuesday–Saturday, 10 a.m.–6 p.m.
Bus: MAX Light Rail, Portland Streetcar, any bus to Portland

THE GROTTO CHRISTIAN BOOKS AND GIFTS

Located on the sixty-two-acre campus of the National Sanctuary of Our Sorrowful Mother, one of the best places to have a quiet read (see "Alone with Company"). Stocks Catholic Bibles and literature.

8840 NE Skidmore St. (at Northeast Sandy Boulevard and 85th Avenue)
503-261-2424
gifts@thegrotto.org
www.thegrotto.org/giftshop.htm
Daily, opens at 9 a.m.; November (after Thanksgiving)–January, closes at 4 p.m.; February–May (up to the Saturday before Mother's Day), closes at 5:30 p.m.; May (beginning on Mother's Day)–

September, closes at 7:30 p.m.; September (after Labor Day)–
November (up to Thanksgiving), closes at 5:30 p.m.
Bus: 12-Sandy Blvd.

IN OTHER WORDS, WOMEN'S BOOKS AND RESOURCES

There were 168 feminist bookstores in the United States ten years ago. In Other Words—founded in 1993 by Johanna Brenner, Catherine Sameh, and Catherine Tetrick—is just one of forty-four left today. Managed by Connecticut transplant Sue Burns since 2002, this nonprofit carries twenty thousand titles by, for, and about women. Also sponsors events and hosts classes and meetings. Model Web site for any community organization. Affiliated with the Women's Studies Department at Portland State University.

8 NE Killingsworth St.
503-232-6003
othrwrds@teleport.com
www.inotherwords.org
Monday–Friday, 10 a.m.–9 p.m.; Saturday, 10 a.m.–6 p.m.;
Sunday, noon–5 p.m.
Bus: 72-Killingsworth/82nd Avenue

LAUGHING HORSE BOOKS

The city's radical bookstore since 1985, Laughing Horse is an all-volunteer, collectively managed store devoted to social change. Hand-lettered signs in the window frame its personality best: "Do we have *Crossing the Rubicon?* You bet! How about Ward

Churchill? Of course! *The Motorcycle Diaries?* Sure! Vanda Shiva's *India Divided?* Yes! *No Surrender?* You bet!" Fiction and videos, too. Offers free meeting space for nonprofits.

12 NE 10th Ave.
503-236-2893
Monday–Saturday, 11 a.m.–7 p.m.; Sunday, call for hours
Bus: 12-Sandy Blvd., 19-Glisan, 20-Burnside/Stark

THE NEEDLE

Benefiting research for juvenile diabetes is this narrow Sunnyside neighborhood shop, just a half block north of bustling Hawthorne Boulevard. Collectible hardback fiction. Operated by David Morrison Books, the shop accepts donations.

1420 SE 37th Ave.
morrison@morrisonbooks.com
Bus: 14-Hawthorne, 15-Belmont

OREGON HISTORICAL SOCIETY MUSEUM STORE

Bring your Oregon history question to manager Andrew VanDerZanden, and he'll lead you to the right book among the store's eight hundred titles. Sections include Oregon Historical Society Press titles and recent issues of the *Oregon Historical Quarterly*, fiction and nonfiction by Northwest authors, natural and cultural history of the Pacific Northwest, and children's books. Store also stocks a big selection of Northwest-themed merchandise: Lewis and Clark, Oregon Trail, and Native American. Don't miss the annual OHS Holiday Cheer and Authors' Party in December, which features dozens of Northwest writers and their books. OHS members get a 10 percent discount on book purchases at the store and at the Authors' Party.

1211 SW Broadway (at Madison Street)
503-306-5230
museumstore@ohs.org
www.ohs.org/store
Monday–Saturday, 10 a.m.–5 p.m.; Sunday, noon–5 p.m.
Bus: Fareless Square; MAX Light Rail, Portland Streetcar, any bus to downtown Portland

PORTLAND ART MUSEUM STORE

Use the entrance between the two buildings to shop without paying admission to the museum. Outstanding selection of illustrated art books and art-themed titles for children. Museum members receive a 10 percent discount.

1219 SW Park Ave.
503-276-4204
museumshop@pam.org
www.pam.org
Tuesday, Wednesday, and Saturday, 10 a.m.–5 p.m.; Thursday and Friday, 10 a.m.–8 p.m.; Sunday, noon–5 p.m.
Bus: MAX, any bus to downtown

TITLE WAVE USED BOOKSTORE

Worth a visit just to see the beautiful Spanish Renaissance Revival architecture, built in 1912 as the Albina Branch Library and one of the county's Carnegie libraries. Stock includes twenty thousand used books, records, CDs, DVDs, videos, cassettes, and magazines. Prices: $2 for hardcover novels and nonfiction. Some items start at 25 cents. Fifty volunteers staff the store, managed by Rodney Richards. Since the store opened in 1988, Title Wave has recycled more than 700,000 books and generated more than a half-million dollars in revenue, and its volunteers have donated 130,000-plus hours. To help, contact Multnomah County Library Volunteer Services at 503-988-5461 or 503-988-5731.

216 NE Knott St.
503-988-5021
www.multcolib.org/titlewave
Monday–Saturday, 10 a.m.–4 p.m.
Bus: 6–Martin Luther King Jr. Blvd.

TRINITY EPISCOPAL CATHEDRAL BOOKSTORE

All proceeds support Trinity Cathedral programs and ministries. The shop serves a wide spectrum of religious traditions, stocking an eclectic mix of books and supporting the activities and needs of the Cathedral community. Serves Episcopal dioceses of Oregon, eastern Oregon, southwest Washington, and northern California. Staffed by volunteers. Offers 10 percent discount to all clergy and to directors of religious education and music.

---

147 NW 19th Ave.
503-790-2877, 1-800-739-6629
bookstore@trinity-episcopal.org
www.trinity-episcopal.org/sections/Bookstore
Monday–Thursday, 10 a.m.–2 p.m.; Saturday, 10 a.m.–noon;
Sunday, 9 a.m.–10 a.m. and 11 a.m.–noon
Bus: 15-NW 23rd Avenue, 20-Burnside/Stark

WILLIAM TEMPLE HOUSE THRIFT STORE

Just east of Portland's stylish 23rd Avenue. Large selection of good-quality hardcovers and paperbacks. Don't miss collectible books inside the glass case near the front door. Donations are accepted Monday through Friday, 8:30 a.m. to 5 p.m. To have your donations picked up, call 503-827-4580. Proceeds benefit William Temple House, 2023 NW Hoyt St., an independent nonprofit that provides free counseling and emergency assistance for thirteen thousand people in Portland each year.

2230 NW Glisan St. (at 23rd Avenue)
503-222-3328
Monday–Thursday, 10 a.m.–6 p.m.; Friday, 10 a.m.–8 p.m.;
Saturday, 10 a.m.–6 p.m.; Sunday, noon–6 p.m.
Bus: 15-NW 23rd Avenue, 17-NW 21st Avenue/
St. Helens Road

Academic

Please call the phone number or check the Web site listed with the bookstore for summer and holiday hours.

LEWIS & CLARK COLLEGE BOOKSTORE

Near the center of this southwest Portland campus, the Lewis & Clark College Bookstore is located on the second level of Templeton Student Center (between Frank Manor House and the residence halls).

0615 SW Palatine Hill Road
503-768-7880
lclark.bkstore.com
Monday–Thursday, 8:30 a.m.–5 p.m.; Friday, 8:30 a.m.–4 p.m.;
Saturday and Sunday, closed
Bus: 39-Lewis & Clark

LEWIS & CLARK LAW SCHOOL BOOKSTORE

The Lewis & Clark Law School Bookstore is located on the second level of the Legal Research Building, just northwest of the Lewis & Clark College campus.

10015 SW Terwilliger Blvd.
503-768-6722
www.lclark.edu/dept/lawbooks

Monday–Thursday, 9 a.m.–6 p.m.; Friday, 9 a.m.–3 p.m.; Saturday and Sunday, closed
Bus: 39-Lewis & Clark

OREGON HEALTH AND SCIENCE UNIVERSITY BOOKSTORES

At the heart of Pill Hill are the OHSU Bookstores (the Medical/Nursing Bookstore and the Dental Bookstore), located on the second floor of the Fitness and Sports Center. Deboard the 8 bus at the hospital on Campus Drive. OHSU owns and operates the stores. Stocks medical, dental, nursing, and allied health books. The virtual bookstore offers a 5 percent discount on most medical titles. Also carries software, materials, equipment, and OHSU-logo merchandise such as T-shirts and sweatshirts. Go Docs!

Second Floor, Fitness and Sports Center, Campus Drive
503-494-7708
books@ohsu.edu
www.ohsu.edu/ohsubookstore
Monday–Friday, 7:30 a.m.–5:30 p.m.
Bus: 8-Jackson Park

PORTLAND STATE BOOKSTORE

Perfect downtown lunch-hour destination: Grab a book and then a slice of pizza from Pizzicato next door and read on the steps next to the Urban Center plaza fountain while the

Portland Streetcar hums past. Founded in 1947 and converted from a cooperative to nonprofit in 2005. PSU students, staff, and faculty can sign up at the store for free co-op membership, which includes a 10 percent discount off all general books and art supplies. Annual member holiday sale in late November or early December offers bigger discounts. On the main floor you'll find excellent reference and writing sections and a large selection of current fiction, nonfiction, and periodicals. Head downstairs for textbooks and school and art supplies. Upstairs offers computer hardware and software. Sale books year-round. Web site features lists of books written by PSU staff, faculty, students, and alumni.

1715 SW 5th Ave. (between Southwest Mill and Montgomery streets)
503-226-2631
mdority@psubookstore.com
www.portlandstatebookstore.com
Monday–Thursday, 7:45 a.m.–7 p.m.; Friday, 7:45 a.m.–6 p.m.;
Saturday, 9 a.m.–5 p.m.; Sunday, closed.
Bus: Portland Streetcar, 12-Barbur Boulevard, 43-Taylors Ferry Road,
44-Capitol Highway, 45-Garden Home

REED COLLEGE BOOKSTORE

Located on the lower level of Gray Campus Center, this non-profit corporation is dedicated to serving the academic needs of the Reed community. Fairly academic focus, featuring university press titles. Best-selling section: philosophy. All trade books sold at 10 percent discount. Order by phone or Internet. The store also buys textbooks and trade books.

3203 SE Woodstock Blvd.
503-788-6615
bookstore.reed.edu
Academic year: Monday–Friday, 9 a.m.–6 p.m.; Saturday, 11 a.m.–
3 p.m.; Summer: Monday–Friday, 10 a.m.–5 p.m.
Bus: 19-Woodstock

UNIVERSITY OF PORTLAND BOOKSTORE

Inside the Pilot House on Waud Bluff (named for Oregon settler John Waud, whose donation land claim was north of the bluff) in North Portland. Campus authors' section, including works by associate professors Will Deming (*Rethinking Religion: A Concise Introduction*), Carol Dempsey (*Earth, Wind, and Fire: Biblical and Theological Perspectives on Creation*), *Portland* magazine editor Brian Doyle (*The Wet Engine: Exploring the Mad Wild Miracle of the Heart*), and Lilah Hegnauer (*Dark Under Kiganda Stars*). Sections include nursing reference, children's books, and general fiction and nonfiction titles. Check out the campus bestsellers shelf.

5000 N Willamette Blvd.
503-943-7125
bksuportland@bncollege.com
uportland.bkstore.com
Monday–Friday, 8:30 a.m.-5 p.m.; Saturday, 11 a.m.–3 p.m.; Sunday, closed
Bus: 40-Mocks Crest

➤ Other Merchants

Although not dedicated to books, the following merchants each offer a substantial number of titles in their respective specialties.

CHILD'S PLAY

Big selection of new children's picture books and chapter books. Knowledgeable recommendations.

907 NW 23rd Ave. (at Kearney Street)
503-224-5586
childsplay@toysinportland.com
www.toysinportland.com
Monday–Friday, 10 a.m.–7 p.m.; Saturday, 10 a.m.–6 p.m.; Sunday, 11 a.m.–5 p.m.
Bus: 15-NW 23rd Avenue, Portland Streetcar

KENTON ANTIQUES AND COLLECTIBLES

Visit this Kenton neighborhood shop to capture the flavor of old Portland. Buys and sells vintage books, comics, and sheet music.

8112 N Denver Ave.
503-285-5077
kingship@spiritone.com
Daily, 11 a.m.–5 p.m.
Bus: 4-Fessenden, 6-Martin Luther King Jr. Blvd., MAX Light Rail Yellow Line

Portland's First Booksellers

Portland, which was settled in 1843, can trace its bookselling roots more than a century and a half, when Oregon pioneer Stephen Coffin—one of the townsite's original owners—advertised in the first issue of *The Oregonian*, on December 4, 1850: "Books and Stationery. A small assortment for sale by Stephen Coffin." (By the way, *The Oregonian* was not Portland's first newspaper. That honor goes to the *Flumgudgeon Gazette and Bumblebee Budget*, a handwritten publication that was published on August 20, 1845.)

Competition came quickly from the San Francisco firm of Burgess, Gilbert & Still, which advertised in the second issue of *The Oregonian* on March 22, 1851, a list of available books and periodicals, including *David Copperfield* and *Harper's Magazine*. Burgess, Gilbert & Still described its capabilities in the next issue of the newspaper, on April 19, 1851: "Country merchants, express riders, and pedlars, can be supplied with all the latest novels, magazines and newspapers, on the most favorable terms. As great inducements will be offered them, they are invited to call before purchasing elsewhere. The only authorized agents of the Eastern publishers."

In the May 17 edition of the newspaper, Coffin announced that he and his new business partner, A. C. Bonnell, in the following week were going to open Coffin's New Warehouse at the corner of Washington and Front Streets, where Coffin, Bonnell & Co. would offer school books, blank books, and stationery.

Another early bookseller was Samuel E. May, who advertised in that same May edition of *The Oregonian*: "A full assortment of Stationery, Noveletts, &c., for sale at Todd & Co.'s Express Office, Portland."

Stephen James McCormick—Oregon pioneer, journalist, editor, publisher, and mayor of Portland—opened the Franklin Book Store in November 1851. According to the 1863 *Portland Directory*, which McCormick published, Franklin Book Store was located at 105 Front Street (at Ash Street). His inventory included school books, miscellaneous books, stationery, and cheap publications.

Two other early booksellers, also listed in the 1863 *Portland Directory*—the earliest compendium of its kind for the city— were Rev. J. L. Parrish, an Oregon pioneer from New York, who operated J. L. Parrish & Co. at 87 Front Street, and Charles Barrett, who operated Booksellers and Stationers at 97 Front Street.

Longtime Portlanders will recall the former J. K. Gill Co., a Portland institution that closed its doors in 1999. John Kaye Gill was a Portland merchant who in the 1860s took charge of a bookstore owned by Dr. W. H. Wilson.

Today, Portland's oldest bookstore still in operation is Cameron's Books and Magazines, 336 SW 3rd Ave. (at Stark Street), which was founded in 1938.

REJUVENATION

In partnership with Powell's, offers new books about home remodeling, house styles, furniture, millwork, Craftsman house catalogues, choosing paint colors, Arts and Crafts. Located on the northeast corner of the first floor.

1100 SE Grand Ave.

503-238-1900

portlandstore@rejuvenation.com

www.rejuvenation.com

Monday–Saturday, 9 a.m.–6:30 p.m.; Sunday, 11 a.m.–5 p.m.

Bus: 4-Division, 6-Martin Luther King Jr. Blvd., 14-Hawthorne

PART FIVE

Borrow Locally: Portland Libraries

▸ Public

AMONG THE BEST EVIDENCE of Portland's love affair with books is the relationship between its residents and the Multnomah County Library, the oldest public library west of the Mississippi and the literal circulatory system of Portland's vibrant reading community. It's the best-used public library in the United States: patrons checked out 19.4 million books and other items in fiscal year 2005.

You need a *Franklin Planner* to keep track of the hundreds of events at Multnomah County libraries: from bilingual story times and puppet shows for children to homework help for teens and English-Spanish conversation practice for adults.

In your mailbox, look for *@yourlibrary*, an eight-page tabloid-size newsletter that is published three times per year and delivered to all Multnomah County households where library cardholders live. *@yourlibrary* includes news about Everybody Reads, the annual community reading project; author appearances; free library programs; Collins Gallery displays at Central Library; bilingual literacy; and special events, such as the annual African-American Read-In during Black History Month each February. Library lovers: Bookmark the Event Finder, the searchable calendar of library activities and classes, at www.multcolib.org/events. For the refrigerator: Each library publishes its own bimonthly events guide, called *Events @yourlibrary*. Watch for the colorful flyers near the entrance to any branch.

Each library is chock-full of resources to help you choose books, chief among them: talented librarians. Don't be shy. They *love* to recommend books. Also, if you love reading lists, look for the library's bounty of brochures on a wide range of interests, from "Northwest Authors" and "Hispanic Voices in Fiction" to "Thrillers Times Five" (medical, legal, suspense, techno, and adventure) and "Writing for Fun and Profit." Frequent updates of these lists—in addition to 125 others, including "Novels Set in Portland" and "A Book for Tomorrow's Assignment" (short reads)—are available online at www.multcolib.org/books/lists. Online lists are divided into categories for children, teens, and adults. Caution: Once you dive in to this section of the library's Web site, you might not surface for a long, long time.

Most of the Multnomah County Library locations offer a free meeting room during library hours for educational, cultural, and informational community gatherings that are open to the public. Seating capacities range from 20 to 120. Apply at each branch: first-come, first-served.

Details about each library follow. For general inquiries, contact the following departments: Computer Help, 503-988-5223; Renewal Line, 503-988-5342; Reference Line, 503-988-5243; Switchboard, 503-988-5402; TTY (telecommunications device for the hearing-impaired), 503-988-5246. Web site: www.multcolib.org; Español: www.multcolib.org/libros.

ALBINA LIBRARY

Opened at its current location—a renovated shopping plaza—in 1999, the Albina Library traces its roots to 1906 and a reading room that housed just one hundred volumes. It became one of the five Carnegies, now the Title Wave Used Bookstore, and then relocated twice before arriving at its Northeast 15th Avenue home.

3605 NE 15th Ave.
503-988-5362
Monday, 10 a.m.–6 p.m.; Tuesday–Wednesday, noon–8 p.m.;
Thursday–Saturday, 10 a.m.–6 p.m.; Sunday, noon–5 p.m.
Bus: 8-NE 15th Avenue, 33-Fremont

BELMONT LIBRARY

1038 SE 39th Ave.
503-988-5382
Monday, 10 a.m.–6 p.m.; Tuesday–Wednesday, noon–8 p.m.;
Thursday–Saturday, 10 a.m.–6 p.m.; Sunday, noon–5 p.m.
Bus: 15-Belmont, 66-Marquam Hill/Hollywood Transit Center,
74-Lloyd District/Southeast, 75-39th Avenue/Lombard

CAPITOL HILL LIBRARY

10723 SW Capitol Hill Highway
503-988-5385
Monday, 10 a.m.–6 p.m.; Tuesday–Wednesday, noon–8 p.m.;
Thursday–Saturday, 10 a.m.–6 p.m.; Sunday, noon–5 p.m.
Bus: 44-Capitol Highway

CENTRAL LIBRARY

801 SW 10th Ave.
503-988-5123
Monday, 10 a.m.–6 p.m.; Tuesday–Wednesday, 10 a.m.–8 p.m.;
Thursday–Saturday, 10 a.m.–6 p.m.; Sunday, noon–5 p.m.
Bus: MAX Light Rail, Portland Streetcar, any bus to Portland

FAIRVIEW-COLUMBIA LIBRARY

1520 NE Village St., Fairview
503-988-5655

Monday, 10 a.m.–6 p.m.; Tuesday–Wednesday, noon–8 p.m.;
Thursday–Saturday, 10 a.m.–6 p.m.; Sunday, noon–5 p.m.
Bus: 77-Broadway/Halsey

GREGORY HEIGHTS LIBRARY

7921 NE Sandy Blvd.
503-988-5386
Monday, 10 a.m.–6 p.m.; Tuesday–Wednesday, noon–8 p.m.;
Thursday–Saturday, 10 a.m.–6 p.m.; Sunday, noon–5 p.m.
Bus: 12-Sandy Blvd., 72-Killingsworth/82nd Avenue

GRESHAM LIBRARY

385 NW Miller Ave.
503-988-5387
Monday–Tuesday, 10 a.m.–8 p.m.; Wednesday–Saturday, 10 a.m.–
6 p.m.; Sunday, noon–5 p.m.
Bus: MAX Light Rail Blue Line, 9-Powell

HILLSDALE LIBRARY

1525 SW Sunset Blvd.
503-988-5388
Monday–Tuesday, 10 a.m.–8 p.m.; Wednesday–Saturday, 10 a.m.–
6 p.m.; Sunday, noon–5 p.m.
Bus: 44-Capitol Highway, 45-Garden Home, 54-Beaverton-Hillsdale
Highway, 55-Hamilton, 56-Scholls Ferry Road, 61-Marquam Hill/
Beaverton Transit Center, 64-Marquam Hill/Tigard Transit Center

HOLGATE LIBRARY

7905 SE Holgate Blvd.
503-988-5389
Monday, 10 a.m.–6 p.m.; Tuesday–Wednesday, noon–8 p.m.;
Thursday–Saturday, 10 a.m.–6 p.m.; Sunday, noon–5 p.m.
Bus: 17-Holgate, 72-Killingsworth/82nd Avenue

HOLLYWOOD LIBRARY

Attention *Ramona the Pest* fans: Hollywood Library is home to the wall-size map of author Beverly Cleary's neighborhood, also available in a brochure if you want to take a walking tour. Landmarks include Cleary's childhood home (east of 33rd Avenue between Klickitat and Knott streets) and Grant Park (33rd Avenue and Tillamook Street), where Henry Huggins looks for night crawlers. Grant Park is also home to the Beverly Cleary Sculpture Garden, which was dedicated on Oct. 13, 1995. Cleary was on hand and spoke about her memories of Grant Park and Grant High School in the 1930s.

4040 NE Tillamook St.
503-988-5391
Monday–Tuesday, 10 a.m.–8 p.m.; Wednesday–Saturday, 10 a.m.–
6 p.m.; Sunday, noon–5 p.m.
Bus: 12-Sandy Blvd., 66-Marquam Hill/Hollywood Transit Center,
75-39th Avenue/Lombard, 77-Broadway/Halsey
Special features: meeting room (50 people), small quiet rooms for one to
two people.

MIDLAND LIBRARY

805 SE 122nd Ave.
503-988-5392
Monday–Tuesday, 10 a.m.–8 p.m.; Wednesday–Saturday, 10 a.m.–
6 p.m.; Sunday, noon–5 p.m.
Bus: 20-Burnside/Stark, 71-60th Avenue/122nd Avenue

NORTH PORTLAND LIBRARY

Special features: Black Resource Center, computer lab, meeting room (85 people), Spanish and Vietnamese resources. The most beautiful interior of the five Carnegies, built in 1913 and renovated in 1999. Don't miss the U-shaped window seat at the south end of the first floor in the Black Resource Center, which houses a special collection of scholarly and popular African-American materials. Look for *Isis* by Charlotte Laverne Lewis on the stairway to the second floor, where the computer lab boasts twelve computers— more than any other lab in the system—that feature Microsoft Office, Publisher, Typing Tutor, and Photo Editor. Call 503-988-4810 to reserve time in the lab, up to one week in advance. Computer lab hours: Sunday, 1 p.m.–4:30 p.m.; Monday, closed; Tuesday, 12:30 p.m.–4:30 p.m.; Wednesday, 12:30 p.m.–7:30 p.m.; Thursday, closed; Friday, noon–3:30 p.m.; Saturday, 1:30 p.m.–5:30 p.m.

Multnomah County Library's Black Resource Center includes more than seven thousand books, videos, CDs, audio-tapes, magazines, newspapers, pamphlets, and clippings that relate to the African-American experience. Works by African and Caribbean writers, musicians, and videographers. Unavailable

BLACK RESOURCE CENTER—The beautifully renovated North Portland Library is home to a special collection of African-American materials.

elsewhere in Oregon: reprints from the Fisk University Library Negro Collection (donated by Michael Powell of Powell's Books), featuring significant historical works (1800 to 1930) by African-American authors.

512 N Killingsworth St.
503-988-5394
Monday, 10 a.m.–6 p.m.; Tuesday–Wednesday, noon–8 p.m.;

Thursday–Saturday, 10 a.m.–6 p.m.; Sunday, noon–5 p.m. Bus: 4-
Fessenden, 40-Mocks Crest, 72-Killingsworth/82nd Avenue

NORTHWEST LIBRARY

2300 NW Thurman St.
503-988-5560
Monday, 10 a.m.–6 p.m.; Tuesday–Wednesday, noon–8 p.m.;
Thursday–Saturday, 10 a.m.–6 p.m.; Sunday, noon–5 p.m.
Bus: 15-NW 23rd Avenue, 17-NW 21st Avenue/St. Helens Road,
77-Broadway/Halsey

ROCKWOOD LIBRARY

17917 SE Stark St.
503-988-5396
Monday, 10 a.m.–6 p.m.; Tuesday–Wednesday, noon–8 p.m.;
Thursday–Saturday, 10 a.m.–6 p.m.; Sunday, noon–5 p.m.
Bus: MAX Light Rail Blue Line, 20-Burnside/Stark, 25-
Glisan/Rockwood, 27-Market/Main, 82-Eastman/182nd Avenue,
87-Airport Way/181st Avenue

SELLWOOD–MORELAND LIBRARY

7860 SE 13th Ave.
503-988-5398
Monday, 10 a.m.–6 p.m.; Tuesday–Wednesday, noon–8 p.m.;
Thursday–Saturday, 10 a.m.–6 p.m.; Sunday, noon–5 p.m.
Bus: 70-12th Avenue

CARNEGIE LEGACY—The St. Johns Library, built with a gift from philanthropist Andrew Carnegie, opened it doors on November 22, 1913.

ST. JOHNS LIBRARY

7510 N Charleston Ave.

503-988-5397

Monday, 10 a.m.–6 p.m.; Tuesday–Wednesday, noon–8 p.m.;
Thursday–Saturday, 10 a.m.–6 p.m.; Sunday, noon–5 p.m.
Bus: 4-Fessenden, 16-Front Avenue/St. Johns, 17-NW 21st Avenue/
St. Helens Road, 40-Mocks Crest, 75-39th Avenue/Lombard

WOODSTOCK LIBRARY

6800 SE 49th Ave.
503-988-5399
Monday, 10 a.m.–6 p.m.; Tuesday–Wednesday, noon–8 p.m.;
Thursday–Saturday, 10 a.m.–6 p.m.; Sunday, noon–5 p.m.
Bus: 19-Woodstock, 71-60th Avenue/122nd Avenue, 74-Lloyd District/
Southeast, 75-39th Avenue/Lombard

► Private

GENEALOGICAL FORUM OF OREGON

Open to the public. This nonprofit bills its library as the largest genealogical collection in the Pacific Northwest: twenty thousand books; two thousand U.S. Census microfilms; fifty CD-ROM databases; and periodicals. Particularly strong in 1840–1870 census records. Carries Multnomah County marriage records. Early Oregon settler files include descendants of Oregon pioneers who arrived before 1900. Annual individual membership: $30. Daily fee: $5 for nonmembers.

1505 SE Gideon St. (north of Powell Boulevard)
P.O. Box 42567, 97242-0567
503-963-1932
gfoinfo@hotmail.com
www.gfo.org
Monday–Thursday, 9:30 a.m.–5 p.m.; Friday, 4 p.m.–8 p.m.;
Saturday, 9:30 a.m.–3 p.m.; Sunday, noon–5 p.m.
Bus: 9-Powell, 19-Woodstock, 17-Holgate, 70-12th Avenue

INDEPENDENT PUBLISHING RESOURCE CENTER LIBRARY

The nonprofit Independent Publishing Resource Center (IPRC) Library, open to the public, houses more than five thousand self-published and independently produced materials, including comics, chapbooks, novels, catalogs, zines, and artists' books. Collection is categorized by subject and alphabetized by title. Also includes a reference section for in-library use, with guides, criticism, history, and how-to information. To borrow materials, register for a library number. IPRC accepts donations to help defray library costs.

917 SW Oak St., Suite 218 (south of Burnside Street)
503-827-0249
library@iprc.org
www.iprc.org
Monday, noon–10 p.m.; Tuesday–Thursday, 4 p.m.–10 p.m.;
Friday–Sunday, noon–6 p.m.
Bus: 20-Burnside/Stark

OREGON HISTORICAL SOCIETY

Open to the public, Thursday through Saturday. Admission free for college and university students who attend Portland Area Library System (PORTALS) consortium schools, including Portland Community College, Portland State University, Reed College, and University of Portland (see a complete list of schools at www.portals.org). The Research Library, located on the fourth floor of the Oregon Historical Society, boasts 35,000-plus titles that focus on the history and cultural heritage of the State of Oregon, the Oregon Territory, the Old Oregon Country, and the Westward Overland Migration. Newspaper microfilm collection includes 16,000-plus reels that cover more than one hundred Oregon cities from 1846 to the present. Vertical File collection maintains more than four thousand subject headings about Oregon history and culture and more than fifteen hundred headings for biographical and genealogical materials. Government Documents is strong in early territorial and statehood periods. Scrapbook collection, created in part as a Depression-era Works Progress Administration project, contains three-hundred-plus volumes, indexed by name and subject. Research assistance—available by phone, e-mail, fax, or mail—is $60 per hour, with a minimum charge of $30.

1200 SW Park Ave. (between Madison and Jefferson streets)
503-306-5240
orhist@ohs.org
www.ohs.org/collections/library
Wednesday, 1 p.m.–5 p.m. (members only); Thursday–Saturday,
1 p.m.–5 p.m. (general public)
Bus: Portland Streetcar, MAX Light Rail, any bus to downtown

POLISH LIBRARY ASSOCIATION

Open to the public. The 1911 Polish Hall in North Portland's Overlook neighborhood houses the Polish Library, which offers books, audio books, and films in Polish, including recent acquisitions from Poland. Also carries books about Poland in English as well as English translations of major Polish writers. Renting of some books and movies is limited to members of the Polish Library Building Association or Polish Library. Film titles are listed online under "Polish Film Club." Don't miss historic St. Stanislaus Church, Oregon's only Polish Catholic church, next door. The two-day Polish Festival in late September celebrates Polish food, dance, and music.

3832 N Interstate Ave. (at Failing Street)
503-287-4077
plba@portlandpolonia.org
www.portlandpolonia.org
Friday, 6:30 p.m.–9 p.m.; Sunday, noon–2 p.m.
Bus: MAX Light Rail Yellow Line

PORTLAND ART MUSEUM, ANNIE AND JAMES CRUMPACKER FAMILY LIBRARY

Imagine reading in the library of a castle. Sink into one of the four medieval revival chairs at the room's center with a J. K. Rowling volume in your hands, and you'll be magically transported to Hogwarts. Welcome to the Portland Art Museum's most-stunning room in the new Mark Building. Thirty-three thousand volumes, stored for two years during the Mark Building renovation, are now available, shelved among the nineteenth-century plaster casts of Greek and Roman sculpture—the museum's first collection, acquired in 1895 by Henry W. Corbett. (Coincidentally, the casts were displayed in the museum's first home, the upper hall of Multnomah County Library.) The Crumpacker Library is a regional resource for the study of art and Pacific

Northwest artists: free, open to the public, and offers reference assistance. Art and history resources for on-site research. Slides of all museum images available. Uses Library of Congress cataloguing system. Current and historical periodicals. Art, artist, and ephemera archives. Vertical and clipping files now catalogued and available on computer database.

1119 SW Park Ave. (at Madison Street), Mark Building, second floor
503-276-4215
library@pam.org
www.portlandartmuseum.org
Monday–Thursday, 10 a.m.–5 p.m.; Friday–Saturday, closed; Sunday, noon–5 p.m.
Bus: MAX, Portland Streetcar, any bus to downtown

THEOSOPHICAL SOCIETY IN PORTLAND

Open to the public. Chartered in 1911, the Portland branch of the Theosophical Society in America—a movement that focuses on the mystical elements of all religions—boasts a library of three thousand items, including books, videos, and cassettes. Subjects include metaphysics, world religions, children's literature, nutrition, and occult fiction. A lifetime library membership costs $10, which includes borrowing privileges of four weeks for books and two weeks for tapes, with one renewal.

2377 NW Kearney St. (at Northwest 23rd Avenue)
503-223-6861
tsportland@juno.com

www.theosophical.org
Wednesday, 6 p.m.–8 p.m.; Friday, 11 a.m.–3 p.m.; Sunday afternoons
during lecture season, November through April.; closed July and August
Bus: Portland Streetcar, 15–NW 23rd Avenue,
77–Broadway/Halsey

► Academic

Please call the phone number or check the Web site listed with the library for summer and holiday hours.

CONCORDIA UNIVERSITY LIBRARY

Open to residents of the Concordia neighborhood. Public users can obtain an off-campus library card at the circulation desk. Located on the second floor of the Hagen Campus Center, closest to Holman Street between 27th and 28th Avenues, the main collection is arranged by Library of Congress classification and supports studies in business, education, nursing, theology, arts and sciences, and athletics. Special collections include the Northwest Center for Children's Literature.

2811 NE Holman St.
503-280-8507
library@cu-portland.edu
www.cu-portland.edu/library
Monday–Thursday, 7 a.m.–11 p.m.; Friday, 7 a.m.–6 p.m.; Saturday,
9 a.m.–6 p.m.; Sunday, 2 p.m.–11 p.m.
Bus: 9–Broadway to 27th and Dekum

LEWIS & CLARK COLLEGE, AUBREY R. WATZEK LIBRARY

Total print volumes: 290,300. Books and other regularly circulating materials may be checked out by Lewis & Clark students, faculty, staff, and alumni. Students and faculty from other area colleges that have established reciprocal borrowing policies with the library may also borrow. See a list of eligible institutions at library.lclark.edu/lib/recip.htm. Borrowing privileges awarded to patrons ($100 annually) of the Friends of the Watzek Library and the Bibliophile Society of Lewis & Clark College.

Special Collections: one of the most complete collections of printed materials on the Lewis and Clark Expedition ever assembled, including books, newspapers, maps, scholarly journals, magazines, pamphlets, and manuscript materials. In 1998, the college acquired the Roger D. Wendlick Collection on Lewis and Clark, which the college calls "the finest collection ever assembled by a single person in the history of collecting books on the Expedition." All copies of Wendlick Collection are first editions, or the same edition copies that Lewis and Clark carried or studied. View high-resolution images of select Lewis and Clark materials online. Special Collections also includes a wide body of books, manuscripts, and broadsides by the late William Stafford, 1914–1993. Stafford, who won the National Book Award in 1963, taught at Lewis & Clark College for more than thirty years.

0615 SW Palatine Hill Road
503-768-7270

circ@lclark.edu

library.lclark.edu

Monday–Thursday, twenty-four hours; Friday, closes at 10 p.m.;

Saturday, 11 a.m.–7 p.m.; Sunday, opens at 9 a.m.

Bus: 39-Lewis & Clark

LEWIS & CLARK LAW SCHOOL, PAUL L. BOLEY LAW LIBRARY

The Boley Law Library, remodeled in 2001–2002, boasts more than 505,000 items, making it Oregon's largest law library. Peter S. Nycum, the present director of the law library, was appointed in 1978. The library was originally housed in Portland's Geisey Building and moved to its present location in 1967. It is named for the late Paul L. Boley, Esq., a Harvard-trained Portland attorney and longtime college trustee.

10015 SW Terwilliger Blvd.

Circulation, 503-768-6676; Reference, 503-768-6688;

Attorney Services, 503-768-6705

lawlib@lclark.edu

lawlib.lclark.edu

United States Patent and

Trademark Depository Library

Monday–Thursday, 8 a.m.–7 p.m.; Friday, 8 a.m.–5 p.m.; Saturday, 11 a.m.–5 p.m.; Sunday, closed. Reference desk: Monday–Friday, 9 a.m.–5 p.m.; Saturday and Sunday, closed.

Bus: 39-Lewis & Clark

PORTLAND COMMUNITY COLLEGE

All PCC libraries have wireless Internet access.

Cascade Library
705 N Killingsworth St.
503-987-5322
www.pcc.edu/library
Monday–Thursday, 7:30 a.m.–8 p.m.; Friday, 7:30 a.m.–5 p.m.;
Saturday, 9 a.m.–3 p.m.
Bus: 72-Killingsworth/82nd Avenue

Rock Creek Library
17705 NW Springville Road, Building 9, second floor
503-614-7413
www.pcc.edu/library
Monday–Thursday, 7:30 a.m.–8 p.m.; Friday, 7:30 a.m.–5 p.m.;
Saturday, 9 a.m.–3 p.m.
Bus: 17-NW 21st Avenue/St. Helens Road

Sylvania Library
12000 SW 49th Ave.
503-977-4935
www.pcc.edu/library
Monday–Thursday, 7:30 a.m.–8 p.m.; Friday, 7:30 a.m.–5 p.m.;
Saturday, 9 a.m.–3 p.m.
Bus: 44-Capitol Highway

PORTLAND STATE UNIVERSITY, BRANFORD PRICE MILLAR LIBRARY

Don't miss this beautifully designed 1989 convex glass building addition, designed around an ancient copper beech tree, on the

Park Blocks in the southwest section of the campus, between Harrison and Hall Streets and 9th and 10th Avenues. This collection of 1.3 million volumes is open to the public, which can use computers on the second floor and kiosk computers throughout the library. Community Account required. Bring photo identification and sign up at the second-floor reference desk. Microcomputer lab on first floor is restricted to PSU affiliates. Public is welcome to use PSU collections in-house. Friends of the PSU Library members (annual $50 tax-deductible contribution, $25 for students) have borrowing privileges. (See www.pdx.edu/library/friends.html for more details.) Bargain hunters: watch for thousands of bargain books, CDs, tapes, videos, maps, and magazines at the book sale each fall, winter, and spring term (early November, February, and June). A bookstall near the elevators offers books for sale year-

REED COLLEGE—Eric V. Hauser Memorial Library, renovated in 2002, boasts nearly a half million volumes.

round. Other special events include exhibits from the special collections and archives and the free Artists and Writers lecture series. Details at the library Web site.

1875 SW Park Ave.
503-725-5874
circ@lists.pdx.edu
www.pdx.edu/library
Monday–Thursday, 7:30 a.m.–midnight; Friday, 7:30 a.m.–7 p.m.;
Saturday, 10 a.m.–7 p.m.; Sunday, 11 a.m.–midnight
Bus: MAX Light Rail, Portland Streetcar, any bus to downtown

REED COLLEGE, ERIC V. HAUSER MEMORIAL LIBRARY

Visitors welcome (by car, enter on Southeast Woodstock and park in the southeast lot; the library is just east of Eliot Circle and south of the Vollum College Center). A sixteen-month, $5.5 million library renovation was completed in 2002. It's worth the trip just to see the stunning brick-walled Gates Reading Room or the narrow spiral-staircase adjacent to South Stacks, both on the Main Level. Houses almost 500,000 print volumes and subscribes to more than 1,700 periodicals and about 1,000 electronic resources. Depository for U.S. government publications. Special Collections and Archives (open Monday, Wednesday, and Thursday from 11 a.m. to 4 p.m. and by appointment) on Lower Level 2: Rare Books (antiquarian maps, A. E. Doyle Postcard Collection); Special Book Collections (including Belgian Collection and Doyle Architectural Library); College Archives (including Champoeg Press, Photographs, Reediana, and Theses); and Manuscripts. Don't miss: Cooley Art Gallery, in the library. Spend at least an hour strolling around the dreamy campus, imagining you're attending one of America's best colleges. Bring a camera.

3203 SE Woodstock Blvd.
503-777-7702, circulation and reserves; 503-777-7554, reference desk
library.reed.edu
When school is in session: Monday–Thursday, 8 a.m.–2:30 a.m.;
Friday, 8 a.m.–midnight; Saturday, 10 a.m.–midnight; Sunday,
10 a.m.–2:30 a.m.
Bus: 19-Woodstock

UNIVERSITY OF PORTLAND, WILSON W. CLARK MEMORIAL LIBRARY

The library on Waud's Bluff will celebrate its fiftieth anniversary in 2008. Named for an Oregon lumberman whose family has financially supported the library since 1979, the Wilson W. Clark Memorial Library houses 350,000 books and journals. Also includes 1,500 subscriptions. Strengths include Catholic theology, philosophy, American history, and Lincolniana. Rare Book Room on the lower level. Services for alumni cardholders, members of Northwest Association of Private Colleges and Universities (NAPCU), Orbis Cascade Alliance, and Portland Area Library System (PORTALS). Guests and visitors who buy a fee card ($15 for three months, $30 for six months, $45 for nine months, or $60 per year) may borrow.

5000 N Willamette Blvd.
503-943-7111, 1-800-841-8261
library@up.edu
library.up.edu
Monday–Thursday, 7:30 a.m.–midnight; Friday, 7:30 a.m.–9 p.m.;
Saturday, 10 a.m. –6 p.m.; Sunday, 10 a.m.–midnight
Bus: 40-Mocks Crest

WARNER PACIFIC COLLEGE, OTTO F. LINN LIBRARY

To the south of Mount Tabor Park sits this fifteen-acre Christian liberal arts college (originally called Pacific Bible College), which moved from Spokane, Washington, to Portland in 1940. Find the Otto F. Linn Library at the center of campus, north of Division and between 66th and 68th streets. Open to the public. Only those affiliated with the college may check out materials. Library contains about 60,000 titles, 300 periodicals, and 1,300 videos. Holdings include reference, juvenile, curricula, and atlases.

2219 SE 68th Ave.
503-517-1102
www.warnerpacific.edu/library
Monday–Thursday, 8 a.m.–11 p.m.; Friday, 8 a.m.–5 p.m.; Saturday,
closed; Sunday, 2 p.m.–11 p.m.
Bus: 4-Division

CONCLUSION

Twenty-five Ways to Sustain and Improve Portland's Literary Quality of Life

IF YOU VALUE THE EXTRAORDINARY QUALITY of Portland's literary life—including seven-day-a-week access to libraries and top-notch independent bookstores, plus availability of locally written and published books and periodicals—then become an active citizen in our city of readers. Here are steps you can take to sustain and improve our literary quality of life while refreshing, renewing, and expanding your individual appreciation:

BECOME A BOOK ARTISAN. Learn letterpress printing, bookbinding, or typesetting. Inquire at Portland Community College and the Oregon College of Art and Craft.

HELP SOMEONE PUBLISH HER FIRST ZINE. Free workshops are available at the Independent Publishing Resource Center.

MEMORIZE A POEM BY A PORTLAND POET. Test the waters with Sam Simpson's "Beautiful Willamette" and continue rowing through time until you reach Vern Rutsala's "Traffic Watch." Practice reciting in the shower, and then amaze your friends at dinner.

UNLEASH YOUR INNER COMIC-BOOK READER. There's a frenzy of comics activity—writing, illustrating, and publishing—in Portland. Join the fray.

READ A GRAPHIC NOVEL. Need a suggestion of where to start? Log on to Multnomah County Library's Web site, click on "Readers," then "Booklists," and then "Teen reads."

WRITE A NOVEL SET IN PORTLAND. Writers, start your engines. Check out the *short* list of novels set in the City of Roses in part two, "Read Locally." There's plenty of room for you.

JOIN THE BIGGEST BOOK CLUB IN TOWN. Catch up with the Everybody Reads titles and watch for the annual choice after the first of the year. See Multnomah County Library's Web site for more details.

ATTEND A READING. There's an author who reads nearly every day in Portland. I double-dog dare you to read the author's book before you go and ask a question at the reading.

WRITE A LETTER TO A PORTLAND AUTHOR. Describe your reading experience of her book. Complain that she killed your favorite character. Invite her to your book group, classroom, or organization.

LOCALIZE YOUR COFFEE TABLE. If you're a business owner, purchase locally written and published books, periodicals, and literary journals for your customers to read while they wait for your extraordinary services. At home, turn your coffee table into a showcase of Portland publishers and writers.

GIVE LOCAL LITERARY GIFTS. Buy everyone on your holiday list a book by a Portland author—there are plenty of titles for readers of all ages—or a subscription to a local periodical or journal. Give tickets to a literary lecture or plan an outing to a literary landmark.

STOP AND SMELL THE ROSES. If you've never visited the John Wilson Room at Central Library, you can't call yourself a Portland bibliophile. The Special Collections are waiting for you.

TEACH A CLASS. Maybe you know Portland's literary history. Share your know-how with others in a noncredit class. Portland Community College could use you.

ENROLL IN A LITERATURE CLASS. This is a wonderful way to reinvigorate your reading life and expand your literary horizons. If you're worried about admissions and grades, online registration is a breeze and auditing is usually an option at local universities.

STEP OFF THE BEATEN PATH. Visit a section at the library where you usually don't hang out. Children's books are not just for children.

RECYCLE. Welcome to Portland. It's a priority here. Haul your old magazines to a hospital. Donate your lonesome books to the Friends of the Library for its annual book sale.

VISIT A LOCAL COLLEGE OR UNIVERSITY LIBRARY. Caution—you might be tempted to take a class just so you can hang out there.

DIG UP YOUR PAST. Find the people who nurtured your love of books—those who helped you learn to read, helped you learn how to use a library, and introduced you to your favorite authors—and thank them. Now pass it on.

JOIN THE LITERARY CONVERSATION. The door is always open at the *City of Readers* Web site. Librarians, booksellers, and publishers can post events there. Book lovers can post photos of local literary interest. Readers can recommend and discuss books. Writers can contribute essays about reading in Portland.

LEARN THE HISTORY OF YOUR NEIGHBORHOOD LIBRARY. Ask your branch librarian about the history of the location.

GET TO KNOW YOUR NEIGHBORHOOD BOOKSELLERS ON A FIRST-NAME BASIS. It helps them remember you and do what they do best: recommend books that are up your alley.

MASTER THE ART AND CRAFT OF PUBLISHING. Portland State University offers a master's degree in publishing, part of the English Department's Center for Excellence in Writing.

CHANGE CAREERS—BECOME A LIBRARIAN. Distance learning makes it possible for Portlanders to earn a master's degree in library science. Investigate the Emporia State University School of Library and Information Management or the University of Washington School of Information.

BUILD A LIBRARY OF PORTLAND BOOKS AT HOME. Every home in the City of Roses should have its own copies of essential books such as *The Portland Bridge Book*, *Trees of Greater Portland*, and *Portland Names and Neighborhoods*.

TAKE A LITERARY WALK. Use the maps in the front of this book to take a bookstore tour, or visit the Oregon Cultural Heritage Commission Web site to see its "Writers of West Portland" map.

Whatever role you play in our city of readers—reader, librarian, bookseller, publisher, teacher, volunteer—thank you for helping to make Portland one of the most vibrant literary cities in the world. *City of Readers* is just a starting point for what I hope will be an ongoing conversation—it would be nearly impossible to list *every* local author, book, bookstore, and resource. If you have a recommendation to share, please join the discussion at this book's Web site, www.cityofreaders.com. Portland is a city of readers. We love to talk to about our favorite authors, books, and bookstores. If you're a reader, you belong here. We're anxious to hear what you have to say.

City of Readers

Designed by Kate Basart
Map and drawings by Steph Gaspers and David Banis
Photographs by Gabriel H. Boehmer
Proofread by Marvin Moore
Composed by William H. Brunson Typography Services
in Phliphilus MT with display lines in Phliphilus MT
Printed by Malloy
on Natures Smooth Antique, 50% PCW